Talking Pictures

Talking Pictures

Interviews with Contemporary British Film-makers

Interviews by Graham Jones
Edited by Lucy Johnson

First published in 1997 by the
British Film Institute,
21 Stephen St, London W1P 2LN

The British Film Institute exists to promote appreciation, enjoyment,
protection and development of moving image culture in and throughout
the whole of the United Kingdom. Its activities include the National Film
and Television Archive; the National Film Theatre; the Museum of the
Moving Image; the London Film Festival; the production and
distribution of film and video; funding and support for regional activities;
Library and Information Services; Stills, Posters and Designs; Research;
Publishing and Education; and the monthly *Sight and Sound* magazine.

Set in Plantin by Fakenham Photosetting Ltd, Fakenham, Norfolk
Printed in Great Britain

British Library Cataloguing-in-Publication Data
A catalogue record for this book is available from the British Library
ISBN 0–85170–603–7
        0–85170–604–5 pbk

For Sarah

Contents

We should treat people well; as if they were real; perhaps they are.

Ralph Waldo Emerson

Foreword

Stephen Woolley

Time and again a producer goes back to the dry well and tries to drink. Doors are slammed, phone calls ignored and scripts returned, but the patient film-maker plods on. Persistence itself can be rewarded. Some people will pay just to get your face out of theirs; some doors will remain permanently closed to the pain in the arse who will not listen to 'reason'. The only motive for the zombie-like existence most producers share is knowing that, at least in Hollywood, the revolving musical chairs tip a different body behind each door every time. A company famous for its children's films is suddenly interested in adult themes. Who would have thought that Disney and Tarantino would make happy bedfellows? A new executive brings new ideas, new schemes and a ray of sunshine – for a limited period only – so there you are, a foot in the door.

As we chase the chances and look for the perfect moment to realise our exciting packages, it is important to remember that the identity of the industry can suddenly switch to anyone's advantage, and this is why this collection of interviews is so timely. This collection will enlighten potential players to the actual state of the game as well as giving the hopeful outsider a thorough description of the stages necessary to take a film to completion.

So many of the conversations mention the struggle, the hard work and the ferocious energy needed to produce 'low budget' and 'no budget' movies, but the reality that emerges is that making any film will throw up a multitude of problems and that getting the money is only the first hurdle in the race to make a film that people will pay to see. There the final sting in this book lies.

It is always a pleasure to read film-makers talking, but of course the essential accompaniment to this collection of conversations is the films themselves. Search them out. Some of them would have been on general release, others have had limited art-house showings, and some of them will only appear on video or on television, but wherever they are showing or are available, enjoy them and only then make up your mind about the state of the British film industry now.

Preface

Lucy Johnson

The publication of this book is proof of the continued dynamism of the cinema, 100 years young. New technologies struggle to assert themselves from virtual reality to digital television but they all look to the movies for proof of where it's at. People often moan about the sad state of the British film industry but these conversations are proof of a newly emerging vitality. Better than that, these conversations show the beginnings of a new European film industry.

The emergence of production funds, such as Eurimages, organised by the European Community, have benefited numerous films mentioned in this book. Pan-European production funds have increased opportunities for a lot of producers but many of the interviewees represented in this book also show an entrepreneurial flair for film-making and often against the odds, with people prepared to live in rat-infested hovels, to sell treasured CD collections, to do whatever it takes to hassle, hustle and haul their baby into the light of day.

For me it is the relationship between the distributors, the marketers and the producer which is crucial as we enter cinema's second century. Film-makers of the next generation need to arm themselves with an understanding of this triangle so their films will reach their target audience. We've got to fill our cinemas with films people want to see and become more actively involved with distribution. Finding an audience is the most important thing.

This book is the idea of a young film-maker who was wondering how to go about making his first feature film. What better way to find out all the angles than to go and talk to those who had done it already? Luckily the intrepid interviewer armed himself with a dictaphone so he could share what he found out with the rest of us.

I am proud to have compiled this collection of conversations between Graham Jones and a very exciting group of British film-makers. It encourages me to look forward to the next 100 years of cinema, in which a revitalised British film industry, emerging in a modern Europe, will be able to compete with other film industries around the world and on its own terms.

Introduction and Acknowledgments

Graham Jones

Conducting the interviews for this book early in 1995 was a process of self-education. I didn't know any of the interviewees personally and as I met them I developed further contacts, more interviewees. It was a very organic and enjoyable process.

I loved knocking on doors and not knowing the person I was about to meet. I came to each individual film-maker without prejudice and asked exactly how they had got into making movies. I told each of them immediately that I believe film-making is a very mysticised thing, that most of us see film-making as something others do and we have no idea who makes a particular film reach our cinema or TV screens. They all agreed and smiled knowingly. On a daily basis for two months, feature film credits became real people.

In one of the first interviews I did I met Simon Sprackling, director of *Funny Man*, and it was he who set the mood for the entire set of interviews. He was attacking what he calls 'The Day I Meet David Puttnam School of Film Making'. It was inspiring to hear from somebody actually making feature films that there is no point waiting around for somebody like David, who will somehow miraculously 'make things happen'. The only person who can get your feature film project off the ground is *you*!

It is all starting to make sense. We are becoming empowered; we are beginning to realise that *we* can do it. It doesn't matter if grant-making bodies don't want to give us funds. The good thing is that people are starting to make films and learning that it can be done without handouts, that film-making, besides being exciting, creative and challenging, can be a viable business opportunity, that money can be made, and sometimes a great deal of it, out of relatively little. We are starting to wake up.

So to all the interviewees, many thanks. To Nina Gluth, the photographer. To Stephen Woolley and Imogen West at Scala Pictures. To Nicholas Johnson for his invaluable help in editing. Film-making is something that happens when people make films, so let's get started.

Dublin, January 1996

Paul Trijbits

'Currently in the UK there are probably ten or twelve producers and production companies that have overhead and umbrella deals. That's new. It's very exciting, very hopeful.'

An independent producer, Paul Trijbits made *Hardware* and *The Young Americans*, helped to develop *Dust Devil* and executive produced *Boston Kickout*. His partner in his London-based company, Trijbits Worrell, is Trix Worrell, who created the TV series *Desmond's*. Trijbits comes from Holland, and studied film at the Polytechnic of Central London before moving into music video production.

Here he talks about the change in recent years in the UK from a situation where films were made entirely independently and no two films were financed by the same people, to one where umbrella deals – in which large media companies provide backing for a series of feature films – are becoming much more usual. Even so, he still has to go to North America for most of the finance for the mass-market movies he wants to make, and fears there is still too little incentive to make feature films in the UK. But with producers like Trijbits based here that may yet change.

One of the most interesting things about film-making in Britain today is the way people use the word 'independent'. It's a bit of a wild goose chase because we're all independent in Britain. In fact, I think every single producer in Europe, is, by definition, an independent producer. The only producers in this country who are no longer independent are Working Title, because they belong lock, stock and barrel to Polygram, and Polygram is either a mini-major or a major.

The image that goes with the term 'independent' is somebody struggling in order to make films. So I think it's important for us to look at that term and ask, 'What does it mean to be an independent producer?' None of us have guaranteed output deals or guaranteed distribution deals that will allow us to greenlight films, unlike in America, where producers work for studios. If they come up with the right goods, the right script, the right creative elements and the right cast the film will be quickly referred to whoever's in charge of the studio, who will greenlight the project so the film can be made. I think it's important to set that out. Independent has two meanings for me. As I said, 'independent' implies struggle: you have no money, you're trying to make your first film. Then there is 'independent' meaning that, for every film you put together, you have to raise the finance from different sources.

How did you become a producer?

I came over from Holland twelve years ago to study at a film school in England, the Polytechnic of Central London. I spent three years there. It was a very interesting course. On the one hand, the school was well equipped. On the other hand, it was rather bizarre in that you had to do a lot of theory that didn't seem to have a lot to do with how to make films. I then spent a year at the National Film School, producing a student's graduation film. This in fact was the one part of my education closest to what film-making is really about, because we had to go and convince the studio, that is the film school, to give us all the money that we needed, to give us all the equipment and so on. You had to go through certain hoops to get your film greenlit. That's where I met my partner Trix Worrell, who's a writer and the creator of the series *Desmond's*. That was about seven years ago. We've been together ever since.

When we started out we got involved in making music videos. That was about the one part of the film industry, including television and everything that goes with it, that seemed to have an entrance level of about nil. Anybody could go in and pretend that they could either produce or direct music videos. Looking back on it, we came in when the music video industry had already peaked and was rapidly going downhill. Lots of companies were going under or were about to go under, but there was still no entrance requirement, unlike with commercials or television where people had to show years of putting in time.

Although the music video production company didn't survive, its greatest assets were a bunch of exciting new directors. Among them was Richard Stanley, who had a real desire to make feature films. I didn't really want to make music videos either. At that point, I knew very little about film-making, I knew even less about science fiction films, which was Richard's expertise. But I loved reading all the books about how to make movies, like Gregory Goodell's *The Guide to Independent Film-Making*.

In one of those books I had read that the great thing about horror films, or horror/science fiction films, was that they could be made for not very much money and that, at least in America, there was a market for them, predominantly on video. So I thought it wouldn't be too difficult to go out and raise the money. Within two months of finding a suitable

4

script we had a deal with Palace Pictures and six months later we were shooting the film [*Hardware*].

How did you get that deal?

In retrospect it all seems rather easy. We just went to Nik Powell and Stephen Woolley and said, 'This is what we want to do and we think we can do it for no money.' They looked at our proposal and said, 'Well, perhaps, but probably not quite as little as you think you can make it for.' They told us to go back and do some more work on the budget. They went out and raised part of the money; we raised some of the money and the film got made. It was really that simple.

Do you think a lot of that was the strength of the idea?

It was the strength of the idea, in a way. But it was also the kind of film that hadn't been made much in England. A few more are now. We were willing to make a film that was technically a non-union film. At that point the union still had some power. The other important thing I think was that the subject and the budget meant that it couldn't really lose any money. Little did we know it would actually make an enormous amount of money in the States. It ended up doing incredibly well in the cinema and subsequently did an awful lot better on video.

I also have to say that I never saw a penny out of the profits of *Hardware*. One of the other problems, when you make your first film, is that the kind of deals that you have to make mean you lose out. But the film got made and it was very successful. We developed Richard Stanley's next film, *Dust Devil*, which we subsequently sold to Palace, and they ended up making it.

A great advantage of being unknown was that I was prepared to do all sorts of things that I would now never do. I would not now be prepared to make a deal like the one I had to do to make *Hardware*. When you make your first film, all you care about is making it. You don't care about eating, you don't care about sleeping, you certainly don't care about getting paid: you just want to go and make your film. The stakes change.

We were also trying to do things with Channel Four. It wasn't so hard to go out and get a bit of development money and go off and try and write a script. I started to look at it a little more seriously and try to work out the kind of films that I was interested in making. Out of that came a desire to make a thriller. When I met Danny Cannon we both found ourselves wanting to make a thriller in London. Out of that came the *The Young Americans*. There is a cultural stumbling block in England. Movies are either considered something crude and American or a vehicle for ideas rather than narrative. The films we are trying to make are for the mass market. Although that doesn't mean to say your film's going to work automatically, *The Young Americans* hasn't worked as well as it should have.

5

But what we tried to do was to make a mass-market film aimed at the British youth audience who otherwise go and see American movies.

You executive produced Boston Kickout *with Danny Cannon. To what extent were you involved?*

I was involved a lot because they were making their first film. I helped them as much as I could without physically producing the film. Everything helps; every film is another feather on your bow. If I'd been sitting here developing thirty movies and not actually making one, it'd be a lot harder to attract an umbrella deal, or to be taken seriously when I go and talk to financiers for whatever film it is that I want to make.

At some point I hope that we won't be dependent on having to go out and raise money from different financiers for every single film that we do. That would bring us to the next stage, which is the position Working Title are in. They don't have to go out and raise the money any more – the money is there. They just have to find all the right elements to convince their studio the film is ready to be made. Currently in the UK there are probably ten or twelve producers and production companies that have overhead and umbrella deals. That's new. It's very exciting, very hopeful. Five, six, seven years ago there might have been twenty producers making films, but they were all truly independent. They didn't have any overhead deals; they were relying on development money from British Screen and Channel Four, the only two sources available. Now you find a group of producers, people like Richard Holmes, Jeremy Bolt and Sarah Radclyffe, who all have the capacity to decide what they want to develop and when. The proof will be in the pudding. I mean, if their films turn out to be films that people want to go and see, the overhead deals will have been worthwhile for these companies.

The other shift that has occurred in the UK is that there is a lot more emphasis on young talent. I'm talking in terms particularly of directors and writers. Look at what happened to Richard Stanley. He made his first film *Hardware* when he was twenty-five. Then he made *Dust Devil*, and now he's now doing a $40 million film for New Line, *The Island of Dr Moreau*. Look at Danny Cannon. He made *The Young Americans* when he was twenty-five. He's just finishing a $65 million film, *Judge Dredd*. I'm doing a film, together with Jeremy Bolt, written by a 24-year-old writer called Stuart Hazeldine, a kind of *Die Hard* on the Underground. It's financed by a French sales company, Pandora.

So how do you go about financially packaging a film?

I've only seen three movie deals in my life, and they were all my own. So I have learnt from the first one to the second one, from the second one to the third one. I do know how it works, I do know my job and I do understand why films get made. I have some theories of my own.

I think that it's quite simple: you need all the elements to be exactly right. That is, one script with one kind of director, and one budget in one fortunate set of circumstances. If one of these elements is not right, the film will never get made. You can go around and try and keep changing the elements, and sometimes the circumstances will change to your advantage. In the case of *The Young Americans* the circumstances changed to our advantage because we ended up working with Polygram and co-producing the film with Working Title. One of the reasons Working Title wanted to do it was at that point they hadn't made a film for nearly a year and nine months and were desperate to make a film. So when I turned up with a film that had most of its money in place, it was a gift for them. But if I'd gone in looking for, say, $10 million it would have been the wrong set of circumstances because they wouldn't have accepted that risk.

To be a producer you have to know two rules. The first is just to go out and do it. That really is the basic rule. You can philosophise and procrastinate and learn everything about how you ought to do it. You can do that for twenty years, trying to find the best way to make a film. But there is no best solution. The only way to do it is to go out and do it and either succeed or fail. Failure can come at any point. Failure can be that you simply don't make the film, or it can be that you make it but it doesn't make any money. Failure can be you make it and you don't know enough about actually physically producing it, so you go over budget.

So rule number two is it's better to make the film than not to make the film. At least you'll have done it.

The next question is: 'Is it any easier when you do it the second or third time around?' As one of the new wave of producers who have done it a few times, I can tell you that it doesn't get any easier, it just gets different. That's the only answer that I can give.

The last thing worth mentioning is that my largest financier, my largest co-producing country, has always been America. I have had more money out of the USA than any other country in the world. I go to America six or seven times a year. Some of those trips are completely futile and fruitless. But I keep going. I keep showing my face, I keep telling people what I'm doing. And somehow you become a part of it. I am now one of the English producers who the American financiers, distributors and Hollywood establishment keep seeing coming back.

A little bit of success along the way doesn't hurt either. In our case, or my case, the success is that the directors that I've found have all gone on to do huge movies. So people think, 'Well, maybe Trijbits does have something, maybe he does have a nose for picking up young talented directors.' So they are prepared to listen. The advantage in America is that it is easier to get things done because there is a constant demand for films. The demand for films in the UK is about minus twenty. There is no incentive to make feature films.

Alex Usborne

'What you find is that some subjects hit a deep nerve. There are some things that go in deeper.'

Alex Usborne is chief executive of Picture Palace North and a director of Picture Palace Films. He is a graduate of EAVE (Entrepreneurs de l'Audiovisuel Européen), part of Media '95, an initiative from the European Community that gave grants to film producers, as well as funding, training, development and distribution. He was also co-founder and first co-chairman, with Jeremy Bolt, of the New Producers Alliance. He has produced four films about Sheffield: *Tales from a Hard City*, a documentary feature film and the only UK documentary to get a theatrical release in 1995, *Johnny Fantastic* and *Brendan's Boys*, both award-winning films about boxers; and *A Band Called Treacle*, a film featuring an all-girl rock band from Hillsborough.

I'm from Sheffield. That's probably the most important thing here. I grew up there, went to school there, played football there, that kind of thing. I always had a talent for words and stories. I went to read English at Sussex University, where there were terrific facilities for making films. There was a television studio and a kit and we just goofed around making many, many films and some of them were pretty good. From that moment on I knew that was what I wanted to do: make films and television, work with stories.

After I graduated I landed a job editing the phone calls on a phone-in programme. It was for a radio station called LBC News radio, which was a 24-hour rolling news station. I loved doing that job and it's probably the best experience I could have had for the job I do now because you have to edit very, very quickly and make decisions about what is interesting and what isn't. What you find is that some subjects hit a deep nerve. There are some things that go in deeper. As a film-maker you always want to look for that kind of stuff. It was a job that kept me going for about seven years, working at night.

Then I hooked up with a director called Brad Langford. We worked together at Greenwich Cable Vision and I had this idea for a show called

Drop in Vision which was a live local-access television show. We did thousands of other films while we were there; just shoot it, edit it, stick it out. But after about a year and a half they realised that they didn't have any viewers, so we got the boot. This was the early 80s, I was twenty-four, twenty-five.

We began making pop videos. We were working for Oliver Smallman, a very successful plugger. What used to happen was that bands would come in and say: 'Oliver, plug our record!', and he'd say: 'Yes I'll do it ... and my boys will make the video!' For a year and a half we were turning out pop videos and I was learning about film-making and also about handling money and budgets.

Eventually I got fed up – it was driving me up the wall – so I decided to go back to stories. I was working with people from the National Film and Television School at the time. I applied to the National but they didn't let me in. They said, 'Stay in the industry', which was good advice. But I did produce two films there: *See You at Wembley Frankie Walsh*, which won an Oscar, and *Shore Leave*, which starred Joanne Whalley and Phil Daniels and was shown at the Metro Cinema. After making those films was the most difficult time. You say 'I'm a producer, I can do it!' but you're effectively unemployable – nobody wants to know. I remember sitting down and writing out my application to be an English teacher, because I thought 'if I can't make films I'll direct the school play'.

And you'd won an Oscar!

That day I got a phone call from two directors I'd known at the film school, Kim Flitcroft and Sandra Goldbacher. They told me about a little film their company had been offered by Network 7, with a budget of four grand. The company they were at didn't want to touch it, the budget was so low. We sweated blood for it, we did two lovely little films for four grand. Immediately they went out, people started ringing us up and offering us commercials. We made one for the *Observer* which was a huge budget for us, about forty grand. Suddenly we were very hot in the world of commercials.

At this stage I wrote a story about a boxer in Sheffield with the Network 7 spin-off, 7-Sport, in mind. I went up to Sheffield to find the boxer but he wasn't boxing any more, he was an alcoholic. Fortunately I found another boxer who had a fight coming up. He was in the film called *Johnny Fantastic*, a great little film I'm really proud of, a really beautiful film. It won two prizes. Almost straight away after that one we were commissioned to make a second film in Sheffield about three boxers, a film called *Brendan's Boys*, which also picked up a couple of prizes.

After that one I wanted to make a longer film about Sheffield. It took me about two and a half years to develop *Tales from a Hard City*, to put it together and raise the money. The idea behind the film was the incredible changes that had occurred in the city, the collapse of the heavy industry and the notion that Sheffield could regenerate through the industries of the third wave: media, shopping, tourism, leisure and sport. I wanted to explore stories that illuminated these changes, stories about survival. I wrote and rewrote and researched and put it all together. It was very difficult to do.

I went on the EAVE Media '95 course where I had a teacher called Jacques Bidou who was a French producer. Jacques was an inspiration to me and still is. He liked the project and the films and wanted to help so he took the treatment to a French commissioning editor called Thierry Garrel at La Sept/ARTE, who rang me up and asked to meet me in Cannes. I didn't have any money at the time, but I'd been getting to grips with all the Media '95 stuff and had applied for a documentary loan, which I got – twelve grand – so I had some money to go down to Cannes and talk to Thierry. In the end he said he'd put his money down. I went back to the UK and I got Alan Fountain of Channel Four and Yorkshire TV to back it. I knew I still didn't have enough money to make the film I wanted to do. The UK had just joined Eurimage, so I asked Jacques Bidou to co-produce it with me, and we were then able to access the Eurimage fund.

We had about £200,000, and we did it, we shot it. It took all of 1993 and almost killed me. We edited and edited and edited and showed a rough version in Marseilles, which is the most important documentary arena in the world. We won the Grand Prix. Since then the film's become a really big success. We showed it at Edinburgh and London, and at the end of April we launched it theatrically. It's a documentary feature film about Sheffield and we're playing it in the cinemas. If it plays for a week and two hundred people come that's already surpassed my wildest dreams. I'm just about to start shooting the next one, which is also set in Sheffield.

Tales from a Hard City II *perhaps?*

This one's called *Heavy Metal Girls*, about an all-girl heavy metal band in Sheffield. I always wanted to be Roger Corman. I wanted to be making these scuzzy little low-budget sexy sassy horror movies and sci-fis, that kind of stuff. I got derailed with the work I'm doing in Sheffield, but I'm really happy with that because I look at all the material and the stories I've got and I know it's got soul, heart and passion, which in the end is the most important thing, for me anyway.

Being an independent producer seems to have given you the scope to tell the stories you want to tell. Would you recommend the independent route to other people who want to tell stories through the medium of film?

It's very difficult to say. There are many different roads and it depends what you want. I am a great believer in the driving creative producer, who is able to have a great deal of control over a project. Corman and Selznick are the style of producer I like. But I think I'm quite lucky in that I am a writer. On the whole I tend to create and originate my own projects. Ninety per cent of the projects on my slate originated from and were developed by me. I'm my own development department, which is a huge advantage.

What do you think of the feeling among younger producers right now? Every interview I do, there seems to be a sense of community, someone knows someone else . . .

I was greatly influenced by the power of the network I discovered in EAVE for producers and film-makers of our age and position. When I first met Jeremy Bolt we just clicked and it was clear that we were talking the same language. It was natural for us to set up the NPA [New Producers Alliance] because we both understood the benefits of co-operating, working together, creating a buzz. And it works, it really does. I bumped into Jeremy yesterday and had a little chat. He's just over the road. We all know each other, we're friends and we share information.

So what would you say to people who aren't in the game yet, who want to make films?

Very tricky to know really. I worked as a runner at the beginning and that's as good a place to start as any. You've got to accept that it takes a bit of time to learn the nuts and bolts. Writing is time never wasted. If you want to be a film-maker you've got to make your first film, a short film of some kind or another. And you've got to make sure that it's good. If you make a film and it's so-so, then nobody gives a fuck, but if you make a short film and it's really good, you will get to make the next one. Because talent, whether in writing, directing or producing, is so rare and if you're able to bring control and vision and energy and excitement, then people will realise it and you'll be able to make your next film, very, very quickly. The important thing is not to rush, to get it right. Make your first film. Any which way you can. And make it good.

The problem is really surviving in the meantime. It's desperately hard. Channel Four isn't a charity. Neither is British Screen. There's not a lot of money around. Having a job in the evenings at LBC was what always kept me going in the early days. It's not a bad thing if you can be a baker or something three days a week, just at the beginning, because it's very hard to survive. It's very hard to look like a successful producer if you're penniless.

If you're doing a nine-to-five job in a different line, then getting into film is really hard . . .

Really hard, but there are new television stations opening every day all around the world and the demand for audiovisual material is increasing daily. It's an expanding market and you have to take heart. There have never been more opportunities. But in the end if you can tell stories with passion and soul and you are able to master the language of film-making, then you will succeed. Because the ability to do that is pretty rare.

Daniel Figuero

'There has to be someone in authority when you're making a film. Otherwise people get very laid back – "Hey, we're making a film!"'

Daniel Figuero grew up in Buckinghamshire and left school when he was sixteen years old to get into film. *A Fistful of Fingers* is a low-budget Spaghetti (Cheddar Cheese?) Western set in Somerset. It is his first feature film as a producer. He discusses the practicalities of film-making, emphasising the importance of having strong administrative backing. In his opinion a phone, a fax and a photocopier are basic needs. Even when you are hustling a film together on a low budget, you must have a responsible attitude. It's important to insure the equipment and get the legal side right. On the other hand, for films with a limited theatrical release, he thinks a sales agent is unnecessary.

I started my film career working for Goldcrest as a runner in the cutting rooms. While I was there I was making short films with other assistants from various Soho-based production and post-production companies. After leaving Goldcrest I went out to New York for a while to work as an assistant director. I then returned to England and was asked to be an assistant director on a National Film and Television School production. That is where I met up with Elisar C. Kennedy who was to direct *Demonsoul*. When the student film had been completed, Elisar and I decided to form a production company to try and get some new, original and unusual feature film projects off the ground.

The first project that we attempted was a wacky story called *Dr Psychedelia*, which Elisar wrote and wanted to direct. It was all about a mad professor who had invented a serum that could turn women into raving nymphomaniacs. We didn't have much luck with that because it was far too weird, no one wanted to get involved with it. Then we got into the idea of making a horror and teamed up with Alex Shandon, a writer, director and producer who'd shot an award-winning film on video called *Bad Karma*. He wanted us to try and turn it into a feature film.

Again, because the concept of the film was so over the top no one wanted to get involved. It was at this point that Elisar wrote another script, *Demonsoul*. After trying just about every source in the UK, we hooked up with a company called Vista Street Entertainment in LA.

How did you get the backing?

Elisar knew some people who had made films for Vista Street before. He'd gone over there to meet the president of the company, Gerald Feifer, who decided to give us the break. *Demonsoul* was a micro-budget film. Our intention was to make an erotic thriller with all the elements needed to sell on video only, which as we all know are unfortunately tits, arse and a bit of suspense. It took us a year to make from start to finish because we were relying on favours for most of it. We couldn't pay anyone, so it was important to keep everyone motivated. We kept saying, 'This is worthwhile, we're making a feature film for an American company.'

If you're making low-budget films, you have to keep everyone's morale up at all times. If anyone starts to fall down, then you have to pick them up and keep them going. If you don't have that commitment, then it all starts to fall apart. To secure locations we had a note going around to the various crew members which said, 'If you know a place where we can film, tell us.' We had about a month in pre-production. We secured all the locations and got some excellent deals on catering and all the equipment.

The thing that almost killed me was when, on the night before we were going to start shooting, the guy supplying us with the camera pulled out. Six hours before we were about to shoot we didn't have a camera! The next morning we lost about three hours going off to hire a camera. In the end we got a very good deal which saved the day. There was another time when a location fell through, and I ran into a telephone box with a fistful of ten pence pieces trying to ring round to borrow anyone's flat. In the end I managed to convince the upstairs neighbour of one of the lead actresses, who was, it turned out, confined to his bedroom with a terrible cold. We shot the scene around sneezes coming from his bedroom.

You become a major hustler doing this type of filming. You've got to be a wheeler-dealer. You've got to adapt to whatever's happening. I hope to do big-budget films one day – it'll be a luxury.

Did you have people helping you, a production manager or an assistant?

I didn't have any assistants, but each department had a head. I didn't need an assistant. What are they there for? To make tea? I can make tea.

The distribution was on video?

It's gone straight to video now in America, Thailand and Singapore.

How much space was there in between shooting Demonsoul *and* A Fistful of Fingers?

I shot *Demonsoul* in February '94. *A Fistful of Fingers* was shot in August '94. In between that I shot *The Audition,* a short film, with a director called Sarah Dutton. *A Fistful of Fingers* was a challenge. I teamed up with the writer/director Edgar Wright. He had raised part of the budget from a local business friend of his. I liked the idea of the script. It's a wacky Spaghetti Western. I love Spaghetti Westerns so it was definitely something I wanted to do. We set up an office in Wells, Somerset, which is Edgar's home town. It helps to make films in areas that the key personnel are familiar with because the locals may pull strings if they know you. I was sharing an office with the ex-mayor of Wells, which was quite weird. At the time he was going through a legal battle with a local businessman, who kept on coming in and threatening to kill him while I was in there trying to produce the film.

The main thing is to have a phone, a fax and a photocopier. A photocopier's bloody marvellous. The amount of paper that you go through is incredible. A whole forest. Get yourself a PC as well, for budgets and stuff like that. There has to be someone in authority when you're making a film. Otherwise people get very laid back – 'Hey, we're making a film!' Someone has to be stern about the whole thing. The shoot ended up being just under four weeks. It's important to see your rushes every day to see where you're going wrong.

Sound is very important. We're doing sound now, patching up all our problems. If you mess up the recording of sound during filming, then you have a hard time at this stage. We didn't do very good sound, so we have a lot of work to do. A lot of sound effects and some ADR [Additional (or Automatic) Dialogue Replacement]. We are also starting to tackle music for the film. François Evans is going to compose the soundtrack, which will be with a full orchestra. I am a big fan of orchestrated music because it can give the film a bigger feel.

There are different types of producers really. Some producers get very involved in it, like myself; some producers are more involved in raising the finance and stick with that.

On your next film will you work with a production manager?

Yes, I'd like a production manager. That would be very good. When you're starting out you try and do everything yourself, the budget, scheduling, everything. That's wrong, there's so much to do, you'll kill yourself.

What about insurance, did you insure both the films?

I had the equipment insured on *Fistful.* My main priority is to get the film done, under budget, on time and looking as good as possible. Insurance costs a lot of money and if you are operating on a micro-budget it is almost impossible to afford it. But I strongly advise producers to get proper insurance for everything, which is what I will be doing in the future.

Do you have to insure the equipment?

You've got to insure the equipment. I paid a fee for the lenses and incorporated within that fee was the money for the insurance. Likewise for the camera. On *Fistful* I got a bit more creative. I wasn't worried about getting it done, I was worried about getting it done properly. At the end of the day if you're making films, you're making a piece of art that is entertainment. I think too many people make the mistake of just going out there and doing it and forgetting about why they're doing it. There is a big buzz at the moment to go out and just do it. But if this new wave is going to succeed, we need to have quality.

How much do you know about selling the film?

I know quite a lot about that. At the moment I'm trying to sell the film myself. I refuse to use a sales agent, because I don't think you really need a sales agent if you do your own trailer. Get a good trailer done and go out to all the main markets and festivals like MIFED [Mercato Internazionale del TV, Film e del Documentario (Milan)], AFM [American Film Market (Los Angeles)], Cannes, Sundance, Edinburgh. You can try and sell the film yourself and you don't have to pay an agent. On larger productions you need a sales agent. But on the smaller productions that are at best going to have a limited release theatrically, you can do it yourself.

We are trying to get *A Fistful of Fingers* to head the Glastonbury festival. I'm going to take it to Cannes and other places. I want to take it to all the festivals and markets. Obviously that costs money but I'll find it somehow, I always do. It's important to have a separate track on the sound dub with only the music and effects so that you can sell to foreign territories and they can put in their language. Make sure you've got loads of production stills and that they're good. The more you do the more you're helping yourself out. I've got a brochure done for *Fistful*, through a favour of a friend. Anything you can do like that, any publicity that you can do, you give it to people, blitz all the journalists with it, try and get ads in the papers. You've got to create your own publicity and try to get as many people as possible knowing about your film.

It says here in the brochure: 'With special appearances from Jeremy Beadle (Beadle's About), *Nicola Stapleton* (Mandy from EastEnders), *Neil Mullarkey* (Comedy Store, Whose Line Is It Anyway). *The landscape photographs in the brochure look convincingly Western-like.*

The reason why we shot a *A Fistful of Fingers* in Somerset was because there are lots of natural canyons there and old quarries. We tried to make it look barren and shoot it in sunlight.

Was the weather a problem?

A big problem. We went over the schedule by four days in the end because of overcast light. I reckon that it was the cinematographer's, Alvin Leong's, most difficult picture to shoot because he needed to have consistent light throughout the whole film. Everyday he would stand there with his light meter, looking at the sky. He had to anticipate when there would be a break in the clouds and how long it would last for. Towards the end I felt sorry for him. So I would look at the sky and give him a countdown for when I felt the clouds would break, and he would be ready with his eye on the eyepiece to turn over. Every evening we would all sit down and make an estimate from weather forecast predictions as to whether or not the next day would be spent shooting interiors or exteriors. As a result, our shooting schedule was constantly being changed and reshuffled. Amazingly, there are no lighting discrepancies in the film. The cinematographer did a bloody good job.

Will the next film be on 35mm?

Hopefully, yes. I don't think much of Super 16. When you want to screen the film you can't have a combined optical print on it, because the thing they do to make it 'Super', to make the frame larger and the grain smaller, is to use the bit where the married optical sound strip normally goes on 16mm. Instead of having two sets of perforations, one on each side, it has one set so the image is larger. But you need to have a combined print to screen it anywhere, so you have to blow it up to 35mm. You might as well just shoot on 35mm, because the money you spend on the blow-up from Super 16 to 35mm is about the same, if not more, than it would have cost to shoot it on 35mm in the first place. However, Super 16mm film is very good if you are going to end up on videotape.

What advice would you give to people who are planning to make an independent feature?

Make sure you've got a good script. If you're going to go out and just do it yourself, make sure you've got a good script. Make sure, if you're intending to cut corners by shooting everything in one shot, that that one shot looks good and sounds good. Quentin Tarantino is brilliant, he's the guy to look to. Get yourself a good producer. I love what I'm doing and the sky's the limit for me. I want to do massive pictures, and the only thing stopping me is the money.

Are you going to work here at Pinewood?

I'm based here at the moment. I'm getting an office over in the main block. I grew up in this area and find it comfortable here. I lived opposite a cinema. I used to go in there and sit in the projection room and watch all the films. The projectionist used to let me cut the trailers onto the beginning of the films. So that's why I got into editing at first. I have tried a bit of directing. But I don't think that's me. Maybe in the future. The creative side is slowly growing on me, and like I said earlier, I'm starting to become more concerned about the way the film looks.

Contracts are very important. The legal side of film-making is very important, because there's a lot at stake in the process. It's very important from the start to have everything secure, to know exactly what people are doing, what they're going to get paid. As you go along you learn about getting a good lawyer, you learn about getting a good accountant. At the beginning, when people first make films, they're so desperate that they forget about the important things. Like where the money's coming from, cashflow and all that stuff. They forget, they just think films, films, films. You learn that as you go along, that you need to have very strong administration. I'm not sure about the people who are trying to do everything themselves: producing, directing, lighting, editing and acting. Perhaps it works for some people. But I like people to have a job and be in charge of that. Everyone works together, they know what they're doing. If anything goes wrong, you know who to turn to. I think it's much better like that.

What do you think of what's happening now in Britain? There seems to be a growing community of independent film-makers.

I think that a few people will pull through and go on to be the new Puttnams. It will always happen. In the 60s there were loads of films being made. Out of that came the names we know today. If someone's desperate enough to make a film, they'll make a film. You hear stories of films that take years and years and years to make, and eventually they come about. If it's a good script it'll happen sooner; if it's not such a good script, then you might need to work on it for a while. Eventually it'll get made. But if you really, really want to make a film you'll make it. You'll find the money somewhere, you'll convince someone because you've got that passion and enthusiasm.

You were involved in Funny Man.

Originally it was called *A Hand of Fate*. I teamed up with a guy called Neill Gorton, who was working in special effects. He was living locally at the time. He'd done *Hellraiser* and all those big horror movies. At the time I was doing short films. I said to him, 'Why don't we write a script together?', with the idea he would do the effects and I would produce it. He wrote this short called *The Family Meal*.

I knew Nigel Odell, who became the producer of *Funny Man*, through his girlfriend. I said to him, 'I've got a script which I've sent to all the TV stations and can't get any money, what do you think, we've got Neill Gorton to do the effects, he's done all these major horror movies, he knows the job. Simon Sprackling can direct it, he's your partner.' Simon Sprackling rewrote it and we shot it in a big old mansion house in Surrey. Neill did the effects and they brought me on as associate producer. I just helped out with a few bits and pieces here and there, put product placement together, got a few crew people involved. What makes a good producer is knowing every single aspect and then standing back and letting people get on with it but knowing exactly what they're doing. In the end Nigel and Simon went on to shoot more of the film, which eventually became *Funny Man*.

Now that I've done really low-budget films, my priority is to look for the exceptional script. You get people like Roger Corman and Russ Meyer who churn out so many films because they've mastered the art. They've cornered their market, they know their market, they know which direction they're going in. Once you know it all, then you can churn them out. But if you want to do quality pictures, which is what I want to do, then you have to spend a lot of time developing scripts. Script is very important. Casting as well.

New technology is always a good thing. Keep an eye on what new technology is happening and then be a part of that. It's always changing. New systems are coming in, new cameras, new stock. Always strive to be in with what's new.

Did you blow up your 16mm footage to 35mm for editing?

No. We're cutting on 16mm but experimenting with various non-linear systems to create some of the sound effects. If we had the money, then I would blow it up now and try to sell it. We have a distributor interested in the UK who wants to put it out on a limited theatrical release using a 16mm print. Then they will do rental and sell-through on video. We also have interest from a television and a satellite company for TV rights. Fingers crossed.

Jeremy Bolt

'We have to make what is happening at the moment a real foundation for growth.'

Jeremy Bolt co-founded the New Producers Alliance with Alex Usborne. A year after graduating from Bristol University he first worked in film as a runner on Ken Russell's *The Lair of the White Worm*. He intends to work internationally as a film producer, with the biggest budgets available, and is part of the 'multiplex generation' whose heroes in the business include Ridley Scott and Alan Parker. He experienced difficulties with the British Board of Film Classification (BBFC) because the content of his film *Shopping*, the story of a young joy rider, seemed uncompromisingly amoral. A producer very aware of the importance of marketing and timing for maximum profit when releasing films, he points out that the delay in releasing his film, caused by wrangles with the Board, meant that on the weekend it eventually opened there was not only a heat wave but also Wimbledon, the World Cup and Glastonbury!

There is a real feeling of community at the moment. Everyone appreciates how hard it is. The deprivation of the last ten years has forced people to work together and be more open. The New Producers Alliance [NPA] is perhaps the most visible symbol of that. It's an organisation established two years ago by a group of young producers intent on making films for large audiences. The credo of the NPA is there are no secrets. I don't know whether my celebrated predecessors would have been as open with each other at the beginning of their careers. Because it's so difficult nowadays we have to be more open. In five years' time whether we will still be as much of a community remains to be seen. People have to work together in order to create an infrastructure that one can seriously call an industry. The more films that are made, the more likely we are to have another success like *Four Weddings and a Funeral*, and the more likely we are to find the new Ridley Scott or the new Alan Parker.

Personally, I don't just want to make films around the £1 or 2 million mark and I have a very specific reason for this. I want to ensure as far as I can my films reach a large audience, and to do that I need big stars and big stars cost money. I also don't want to be poor and it's very difficult to make money on a film that costs £1 or £2 million. From a producer's point of view you make your money in the production budget. The higher the budget the higher the fee. The more money you make, the more money you have to invest in scripts and development. You have more chance of building a company. Perhaps that has been lacking in producers in the last ten years in the UK.

I have a business training background as well as an arts background and I sense a similar attitude among a lot of the young producers. Paul Brooks used to be in property; Paul Trijbits is a very aggressive commercial animal; Richard Holmes, the co-chairman of the NPA, is a very aggressive commercial animal. We're not precious about our art. We have to make what is happening at the moment a real foundation for growth, rather than a flash in the pan, because previously that's what it has been.

The fact that in the generation above me there are only five or six producers actively working is ridiculous. There needs to be in every ten-year generation at least twelve to twenty who are active before you can say you have an industry. It shouldn't just be Tim Bevan and Eric Fellner, Stephen Woolley and Sarah Radclyffe. There has to be more than that and I hope that in our generation there will be at least four times that. Then I think you'll have a real industry. When I started out I was also only concerned with getting the film made, but when you see that money can be made at something, you sure as hell try and make some.

What was it like on the first day of shooting Shopping?

I think I was on set around six – before anyone else. I remember just being amazed at the number of trucks there were. I had to go out and keep counting them. That to me was the most exciting thing, just seeing all these huge vehicles with masses of equipment. The other thing I remember was the catering. We were very nervous that the catering wasn't up to scratch.

What level of contact do you like to have with a film crew?

Well, what I try to do every morning on a shoot is to see all the heads of department. I like to be on the set. I have a line producer I work with who's terrific, but I like to be with the director. I don't see what the point is in sweating blood, spending half the year on the telephone, if the one chance you have not to be on the telephone, you stay on the telephone. I like to see the film being made. The film is made on the floor and in the cutting room. So as a producer you have to have a technical understanding. If you don't, you're not going to be able to do the budget, you're not going to be able to understand the location manager's problems or the assistant director's problems. You can come into producing simply as a financier. But the real fun has to be on the floor, getting your hands dirty.

How long was the shoot?

The shoot was eight weeks. We had twelve weeks of post-production, a two-week dub and an eight-week prep. We were very prepared and we have a very clear idea of what we were trying to do. We had enough time to work it out. It'd taken me four years to get the thing together. To that extent it was calculated. Paul Anderson, the director, and I are firm believers in selling ourselves.

Film is a very public business. You have to publicise yourself to publicise your film, and we thought a lot about how we were going to get the film across to an audience with music and fashion. You're not just competing with other films in the market-place, you're competing with other activities and other lifestyles, you're competing with restaurant, the health club, the swimming pool, the night club, late-night football. Everything else that's out there.

The film reviewer Todd McCarthy said of the directors of Shopping *and* The Young Americans *that, 'These would-be rebels without a cause will remain rabble without applause.' What do you think of that?*

Both directors have gone on to direct some of the biggest films to be made last year. Paul [Anderson] is going to direct one of the biggest films to be made this year. He's not yet over thirty. You can't have a rabble mentality and achieve that kind of success before twenty-nine. Danny Cannon, the director of *The Young Americans*, is twenty-six and has handled Sylvester Stallone.

I believe that film-makers should reassess the kind of films they're making and producers should be as imaginative as possible as to where they get the funds. *The Stars Are My Destination* is a $50 million science fiction epic developed by a German company, Constantine Films. Paul Anderson will direct it, I will co-produce it and I will endeavour to make sure it's shot at Pinewood or Shepperton. I need therefore to get good deals out of Pinewood or Shepperton. They have to be able to compete with the studios in Germany and indeed LA. That's not subsidy, that's competition. That's healthy.

How did Shopping *do at the box-office?*

It didn't do very well. It did better in Newcastle and the north of England. It did alright in London. It came out on a very bad weekend, a weekend with a heat wave, Wimbledon, the World Cup and Glastonbury.

We were completely out of sync with our publicity campaign because the BBFC didn't give us a theatrical certificate in time to hit our March date. We had a number of problems that have taught me a great deal.

Frankly I wouldn't want anyone to go through those difficulties with their first film; it's very disheartening when you've put so much effort in. When you're a producer the idea is that you're in control of everything. You're not in control once the film's been delivered. You never find out what's going on. Not unless you control your own distribution as Palace used to do in the UK can you really have muscle as a producer. It's a very enviable position that Stephen Woolley and Nik Powell were in.

What's your perception of the BBFC?

I think that James Ferman [head of the BBFC] is in an inevitably compromising position because he is a political football. On the one hand, he doesn't want to get too close to the film-makers for fear of being compromised by his relationship with them. On the other hand, the lobbying that is thrown his way by Parliament means that he is maybe too close to the politicians, who are completely out of touch with the film industry. The BBFC is a body with tremendous power; it doesn't appreciate the commercial power it has over film-making. The fact that *Shopping* was delayed because it didn't get a certificate on time probably lost Polygram 50 per cent revenue on the movie.

James Ferman probably isn't even aware of that. Why should he be? His concerns are more political. One the one hand, the Conservative government are meant to be the great protectors of the free market. On the other, they are simply using the BBFC and the censorship issue to force the real issue away from their own incompetence and direct it against film-makers. There's too much political pressure on James Ferman and it's distracting him from his responsibilities to the film industry. I don't think he would choose to be in that position. I do have every sympathy with him. I would point the finger very firmly at the government.

Did you take the film to Sundance?

Yes, we did. It was great fun. It's a great opportunity to meet young film-makers. You can bitch about the industry, be attacked by various agents. It's very recreational, Sundance. It's more about agents finding the new Tarantino than producers making deals. You generally go to LA after Sundance to close the deal. If you're invited to Sundance, you should have a good time. That was certainly our attitude, we had a chalet, I had half the cast there, we had a ball.

Once you've made your first film things get a little bit different. I've got over that anxiety of just having to make a film. With the first film it's just important to get it made. With the second and the third film you can go for the money, the awards and the critical acclaim. Pressures change. But

I think that there's no big secret about how one does it, there's nothing special about having produced a film at a young age. It's just a question of doing nothing else for four years. Most of my friends who've produced movies when they're in their mid-twenties have really nothing else in their lives. That's not necessarily a good thing. Young people have a certain kind of energy. But it doesn't really matter when you do it, as long as you do it. It took Jeremy Thomas thirteen years to raise money for *The Last Emperor*. Tarantino got it right the first time round. James Cameron was an art director and a production designer before he got his break.

At the end of the day producing is about energy. Directing is about having to make extraordinarily difficult choices constantly. Producing is about diplomacy and energy. Being able to handle people. In my limited experience, that's what I've observed. If you believe it enough and say to people 'it's brilliant' enough times, somebody eventually will believe you and give you the money. Once you make one, you can relax a bit, focus on the next one and start thinking how to build your company.

You don't get a great deal of recognition from the public and you certainly don't get the money the directors and the artists and the actors get. You don't get the creative satisfaction the directors and the writers get. There's a lot of pain. It's very difficult to have much else in your life. Late nights. Early mornings. You have to really love film.

Elisar C. Kennedy

'Okay. So what if there is a crisis?'

Elisar Kennedy has been working in the film business since the age of seventeen when he was a production assistant on a low-budget movie in LA. Returning to London, Elisar teamed up with fellow film-makers to try and kick-start commercial low-budget film-making in the UK. *Demonsoul*, which he directed, was the product of a connection with a production and distribution company based in LA. After *Demonsoul* Elisar produced *Virtual Terror*, a horror anthology. He is currently working in the acquisitions and development department of an international sales company. The British film industry may lurch from crisis to crisis, but Kennedy believes you have to ignore this and just get on with making films.

It's like anything creative. If you are prepared to spend years on poverty row, it's entirely up to who you are and what you have to offer. It's not like going to a school and passing an exam and having a qualification. You don't need any qualifications for film-making. That's probably why I knew while I was studying my A levels that I wasn't going to go to university. I didn't feel I had to; I knew I wanted to work in film. There have been members of my family who have been working in film. I guess they've acted as inspirations for me.

When I was seventeen I went out to LA and pulled whatever strings I could through my family to get a job as a runner on a film set. Once you're on a set, it confirms whether you want to do it or not. There's nothing to beat working on a film set. It's one of the most thrilling experiences, although it's hard work and a lot of the time it can be very, very boring. Starting out as a runner and as a production assistant, you do jobs that you never do anywhere else, in any other kind of work. At the end of the day you feel satisfied that you've made a contribution to the making of a film, even films that no one has ever heard of! I was working on really low-budget productions, which are made by the dozen in the States, in LA specifically.

I didn't want to do film school partly because I've volunteered on films at the National Film School, and I've seen students who have been hanging around there for years on end. It's supposed to be a three-year

25

course, but you see students who are there five, six, seven, eight, nine or even ten years later and they still haven't left. They feel there's no reason to go outside the film school. They can't get out, because outside in the real film world it's very cruel. At least they have some kind of security there.

The independent very low-budget films I was working on in the States are made for about £350,000, which is not a lot of money. But it's enough to be able to do three- to four-week shoots and make a film that's easily sold. They pay people, there is none of the deferment that they have over here in the UK. It's something I've always thought that we should try and bring over. I haven't felt there's been a need for a lot of the deferment films they've been making over here. They've had budgets to make a film that they intend to sell so it should be possible to pay people.

Demonsoul was different because the budget was so incredibly low and I was making it for an American company who owned it. I knew that there wouldn't be any profits. To offer deferments would have been dishonest. With *Demonsoul* everybody worked on a voluntary basis. It was quite clear that there wasn't going to be any money for anyone at a future date, so there was no point offering it. I have done deferments and I have worked for very, very low wages. Personally I think I would prefer to work for a very, very low wage than have the promise of more money later. That very low wage is cash in your hand. What you see is what you get.

Working on those films in LA was my experience of learning the ropes of film-making. I got to work my way up from working as a production assistant, to working as the actual assistant to the producer. I got to see first hand how budgets were put together. I was given scheduling assignments, and I would help schedule with the assistant director and the production manager. I got to learn the nitty-gritty of being behind the scenes producing the film. Working with low budgets, being in that position, you learn a lot. It's one of the best experiences that anyone could have for learning the ropes. A lot of the time you'll be offered really bad assignments which seem really shitty and boring. But they have to be done.

The film-making community is very, very small. So people get to know you. If they know that you'll do the work and you're good at it, then they'll come to you to do the next picture. It may not be a lot of money again, but you start developing friendships with people, you start meeting people. I noticed in LA that everyone on a film set had a script they'd written or were putting together. They're all waiting for the right moment, when they'll meet a sympathetic producer who'll actually read that script. To get into the industry, the best things to do are to develop relationships with people and prove that you're enthusiastic, that you'll do the work.

As a PA you learn when you're on set that you should never, ever sit down. If you sit down you look lazy. So you've always got to be standing up and hanging around, asking questions. There's always something that can be done. You're not going to get the day's work done unless everyone's done what they were supposed to do.

Before I began these interviews I hadn't realised the effect that Corman has had on film-making. Is he someone we can all learn from?

I think so. I don't buy into the recent British film-making 'Brit Pack' thing. They've been calling themselves the 'multiplex generation', saying that their heroes are James Cameron and so on. To look to the Hollywood style of film-making when you are an independent film-maker is ludicrous. How could they possibly be role models when they're working in an entirely different situation? When you make a movie in Hollywood, you have a script which goes up to the chairman of, say, Columbia. You pitch them your project, they'll read it, then they'll greenlight it. They'll invest, say $60 million in a project, of which maybe $15 to 20 million is the studio overhead.

It's not an entirely creative process. The director of those Hollywood movies may not have been attached to it at the script stage. It may have been given to the producer by an agent, who says he must use a certain director if he wants to use certain cast members. The producer who has found the script and has been trying to put it together for so long might not agree that they are the best choice for the script. But he doesn't have a choice. They come as part of the package, which is the only reason that the studio will give you the money to make the film.

As an independent, you have to find the script, you have to put together the finance. Usually you have a director that you want to work with. A lot of the time, the writer is the director as well. You don't get writer-directors in the Hollywood studio system, because the writers usually work in-house. They are writing scripts the whole time and perhaps one will get made every five years.

So yes, Roger Corman is one of the biggest influences on independent film-making. Certainly he proved that you can make a commercial product on a low budget. A lot of people you meet will have worked for Corman, a lot of people go through his studios. I was offered a job as a second second assistant director on a Corman picture. You work for them on a first picture in that job and the actual second assistant director gives you training. On the next Corman picture you work on, you're the second assistant director. And so on, until you become the first assistant director. Then, if your ambition is to produce or direct, you work your way up through the ranks. A lot of the assistant directors and line producers I met in LA had gone through the Corman studios, working on two, three, maybe four pictures.

To make Demonsoul *you went to the president of Vista Street Entertainment and asked him for a break. Could you tell me about that?*

I'd known about Gerald Feifer, the president of Vista Street Entertainment, for some years. One of the producers I was working for on a couple of pictures, Matt Devlin, had done a couple of movies for Vista Street. They were low-budget 16mm exploitation films. They are a bit like Corman Studios. A lot of the people I met had done a film or two films for Vista Street Entertainment. It was only natural to try them out when I decided I was going to make a film.

Gerald knew a lot of people that I knew and was willing to put money into a low-budget commercial project. He makes lots of films every year. They're either sexy comedies or horror films or low-budget action films. I sat down and wrote a script and sent them the various drafts. They liked the way I wrote. We developed the *Demonsoul* project. They would send me faxes back, recommendations for the next draft. We worked quite closely on it. So we got to a stage where he loved the script, thought it was a great project and wanted to make it.

In summer 1993 I went out to Houston to work on a film. I was working in the art department, in a heat wave, on a Charlie Sheen movie called *The Chase,* which got a very brief release in the UK. After that wrapped I took a plane and went over to LA to talk to Gerald about *Demonsoul.* He was enthusiastic, he wanted to make it. He was thinking of making it with a slightly higher budget than normal. On his slate of films, there's usually one quite a bit higher budget than the others, like the *Witchcraft* series. He's now made seven of those. I think only one and two were ever released in the UK.

He asked me, as an alternative to *Demonsoul,* if I would write some horror ideas, which would be very low budget. I could write and direct and produce one of them. I wrote him a couple of treatments, and he liked them. I was only staying in LA for three weeks, so the day I was leaving, on my way to the airport I stopped off at his office and said, 'Look, what about *Demonsoul*? Let's make it.' He agreed, wrote me a cheque and I rushed off and cashed it immediately.

What was the money for?

It was to cover my pre-production expenses for scriptwriting and development. Then I would go back home and start production. He would send the production cheque through the post. So I got on the plane, went home and started planning *Demonsoul.*

I met up with Danny [Figuero] who had been trying to put together a short film which had fallen through. Danny and I had worked previously on a project which didn't happen. I asked him to join me on *Demonsoul* as a producer. As the writer and director, trying to produce the whole film would have been too much work. It was good that Danny came on board; it took a lot of weight off my shoulders.

Spring 1994 we went into production, with Vista Street paying all the costs. They sent the money through; it was up to us how it was going to be spent. But we knew that they had bought the script: it was their project, it was their money, it was their film. Even though it wasn't a lot of money the important thing was to remember that, if we kept within budget, then at least we wouldn't be spending our own money. We wouldn't be making money but at least we wouldn't have lost any. It was fortunate that I had got an American company to pay the bills. I could make a first-time film, and it would get a video release in the States courtesy of Vista Street Entertainment.

Certainly there are not a lot of people who can say they've made a film that's going to get a US release. It's not a great project by British film standards. It's a horror B movie; it was designed to be that. It's the sort of movie that a lot of independents make in the States, churn out and make a quick buck on. Having liked those movies I was glad that my first film would be a vampire film. It's a hip thing now, vampire movies, so it's nice to be able to ride a bandwagon. It probably won't be released over here.

I think the UK is a hard market to crack because they're very particular as to what films they like. Certainly they don't have the range available on video that the States or countries like Holland or Italy do. It was a slog only having a two-week shooting schedule to do an eighty-minute film. That's normal for the States, but here in the UK people think that a five- or six-week shoot is normal. On a low-budget project there's no way you can do that.

One of the good things about the film is that we had really, really good actors. All English. I think they all have a great future ahead of them, they're very talented. I'm glad to have had the chance to work with those individuals.

Most people say that the first film is a hell of a learning curve.

Having worked on low-budget films in the States it didn't seem – even though I was directing – that much of a progression. I do believe that film-making is teamwork. The fact that I was directing *Demonsoul* didn't seem to make a difference. We were all making the film and everyone was making a contribution. There are some directors who are auteurs; I certainly am not. I would never want to be, nor would I ever claim that *Demonsoul* was any kind of auteur movie, even though I'm the producer, writer and director. It was shot the best way possible to make it on budget and on schedule. That couldn't have been done if everybody hadn't been working together.

If you're making a low-budget film, be prepared. One of the best ways to be prepared is knowing how to schedule. Two weeks is a pretty good schedule to be working with when you're working on a low budget, and you're not paying anyone. You're not filming long enough for people to start hating what they're doing.

There were days you couldn't possibly predict and things inevitably went wrong. We had one great location that we wanted to use for an office sequence, a three-day shoot. For the first half of the first day we were just working out all the sound problems we had. We were getting buzzing noises, we couldn't work out where they were coming from. It was probably something to do with the location. We were getting some interference on our sound recording, consequently everything on it was crap. Halfway through the day we had to make the decision to go over to my house to film there instead. All the equipment was packed up again and driven over to my apartment. That was half the day wasted.

It's about working with people, working with the cameraman, working with the director of photography to find out where you can save time. We did it, we did the three days' work in two and a half days. We didn't get every single shot that we had to get, but we got everything that was necessary. Which is the important thing if you're making a film. Certainly I had to lose a bit of artistic directing in order just to get particular scenes finished. If you are behind schedule, then you're possibly going to lose whole sections of the script, because you just can't get round to filming them.

It was especially difficult because one of my main actors was also appearing in a theatre play and had to rush off at six o'clock every day. He was one of the main leads. No only were we half a day behind on that location, but we weren't getting one of our main actors for that scene for the whole day. But if you're working with good people who are fast and know the job, they can show you where you can save time and get the job done.

It was a tough shoot. Though we weren't doing long days for a lot of the days. We were doing maybe nine or ten hours, which is very reasonable for an independent low-budget film. There were things like shooting in a park where we ended up getting thrown out because we didn't have a permit.

Personally, I don't think I'm a director. I think I directed the whole film from the point of view of being a producer. That is what I want to do now, to produce rather than direct films.

What do you think of the independent sector in Britain now?

There hasn't been a time in British film history when there hasn't been some kind of crisis. What the so-called new wave of film-makers, which I guess includes myself, have cottoned on to is 'Okay. So what if there is a crisis? What's the point of going on about it?' People realise now that the only way to get your first film off the ground is to go out and make it happen.

Sam Taylor

'The British film industry is only as good as its ideas and energy.'

Sam Taylor went to Manchester University where she studied English and American literature. She worked for a foreign sales company, Oasis, where she sold, among other films, Peter Greenaway's *The Cook, The Thief, His Wife & Her Lover* and *Prospero's Books*. Frustrated by the lack of long-term job satisfaction in sales, she left Oasis in 1994 to form Mass Productions with investment banker Mathew Wilson, where she produced *Before the Rain, The Young Poisoner's Handbook* and *Sweet Angel Mine*. In this interview she remembers how working in foreign sales led to her becoming a producer of a particular kind of film.

I wasn't one of those people who always wanted to work in films from when I was little; I didn't sit there when I was eight saying, 'I want to be a film producer'. I was travelling a lot when I was about twenty-three and I wanted to go to Cuba. I met a friend of mine who worked in a distribution company and I was desperate to get some work, just for three weeks, over Christmas so I could make some money. They had a job in reception. After Christmas I decided to stay another two weeks and then I got promoted to being the managing director's personal assistant. I stayed there being his PA and the company started to go into world sales. In the end I was managing that side of the company: Head of International Sales. We were doing Peter Greenaway films. We did *The Cook, The Thief, His Wife & Her Lover*.

How do you go about selling films?

You go to every film market like Berlin or Cannes. Once you're out there you just set up your office and you sell the film. It was very good because you get to meet all the buyers across the world. You learn why they buy certain films and what they're looking for and about their own problems. I think a lot of independent producers have got a real hatred of distributors, thinking that they're bastards who cream off all the money. Some of them work really hard just to get your film out in the best cinemas. They have to go through the process of convincing the local cinema people to put the film on. We used to get to the market, read through the listings of who was there, check on what they'd bought before to see if they were the sort of company that would want a Peter Greenaway film.

It was very good training for me because it's similar to the process of producing: I go and look at what people have been involved in before to see if the film I want to produce is the kind of thing that they would be interested in. It's like going for an interview, you do the research before you go in.

So when you're choosing projects, you know when you can go to certain people?

I have a very good idea. When I'm reading scripts I know sometimes that I can get a bit from here and a bit from there. I've been offered films that I'd really like to do, but I know they would either take too long to finance or I just couldn't get the money for them. To be a producer you have to have that ability to look at somebody else, work out what they want and then give it to them. You're not asking them for money, you're giving them something that they need. That's the kind of mentality you have to have when you're going to them. It's very important.

When I was in sales we presold *Prospero's Books* to a Japanese company. I had a faint idea that this was similar to what producers did; I didn't really know anything else. I was getting very tired of sales because sales is a very quick high. You feel really good for a while but at the end of the day it's just another sale. I wanted to do something that you could get more long-term satisfaction from, where you felt that you have seen a project all the way through.

A lot of sales people act as if they made the film, which is ridiculous. I was friendly with an Irish producer at the time and we were talking on the phone one day and he said he was going off to Russia to make a film, an Irish–Soviet co-production. I said, 'I'll come too, I'll do anything!' I was joking on the phone, but I actually really did want to get out. Then he rang back the next day to see if I was serious. I was earning quite a lot of money at the time and he was offering me, I think, £75 a week. I was on about £1,500 a week then in sales, but I knew I wanted to do it. I went to Russia and it was just mad; very, very low budget. I had never been on a set before. Someone gave me a book, one of those books on how to make a film, and told me I was third assistant director from Monday. I was studying all the call sheets and trying to work out what I was doing.

We went in August and it was hot, then it got colder. People can't film in Russia after about November because the film freezes up. It was a film about three lesbians. But the Russian people wouldn't admit that lesbians existed. They'd say, 'What's the film about?' and we'd say, 'It's about lesbians', and they'd say, 'What's a lesbian?' The film went to Ireland for post-production and I decided I wanted to see it all the way through so I said I'd do post-production.

I came back from Ireland. A merchant banker who I knew rang me up and said he was setting up a film company, and asked me to come and work with him. That's the company where we started to get *Before the Rain* together. The first year you never get anything made. You sit there feeling you're never going to make a film, that it'll never happen. It seems like an impossible goal. We were lucky to get development money, little bits here and there. But the idea of actually making a film seemed so far away, we never thought we'd get there. This was in 1992. We were developing different things, low-budget things mostly.

You didn't miss being a sales agent?

No. People get burnt out very quickly in sales. You never stop working. You go to a party in Berlin, but you're not at a party. You've got to find a particular person and make sure they come in and see you the next day so you can make a sale. We had a very nice boss, but if you don't hit the target, like in any sales, then you're out. It's a very high-pressured job. If you don't sell everything you have to sell in a week then you don't have a job any more. It's really not a nice job.

At the time I wasn't interested in people like directors, I wasn't interested in producers. The interest was in people who could buy the films the company had to sell. The whole perspective on the industry was different. You might walk into a room and see David Puttnam. Of course, you were interested in meeting him but you were much more interested in meeting the man who could buy your film.

Tell me about your first film, Before the Rain.

It was a script from British Screen, who had developed it. I'd read it about a year before. It was easy to put the money together because there were only three companies involved: Channel Four, PolyGram France and British Screen. The finance came together very quickly. The shoot itself was very, very difficult because we were shooting out in Macedonia. We were there for seven weeks and three weeks here. It was a long process. Now it's been nominated for an Oscar, Best Foreign Film. Which is weird, because the process at the time was so desperate.

So you'll be going to the States soon?

Yes. I've just been in America for Sundance. I thought Sundance would be quite relaxed. I went over there thinking we'd all sit around drinking herbal tea and talking about angles but it wasn't like that at all. It was mad. It was like being in LA. You'd be invited out to dinner, sitting in a restaurant and people would start doing this table-hopping thing, so you'd end up having dinner with about six people. We went with *The Young Poisoner's Handbook*. It was the first time it had been shown to anybody and people were giving it so much hype: some people were saying, 'It's the best film I've ever seen.' I think it's a very good film but it's not the best film in the whole world ever.

Does the fact that you had two films at Sundance mean it's going to get any easier for you?

It will help. But I know we're going to be in the same position for the next film when we're looking for the money. It's not going to suddenly mean I get offered millions of pounds by Paramount.

Paul Trijbits was talking about how one defines independent. He pointed out that everyone in Europe is independent because for each film you have to go to different places for the money.

Each film needs different types of money. For example, the film that we're working on at the moment is called *Sweet Angel Mine*. It's a horror story so it won't get money from the same sources as *The Young Poisoner's Handbook* or *Before the Rain*, because it's a different kind of film, a different genre. That's the excitement of it. Still, all the films I want to make are intelligent and provocative; perhaps that's a genre in itself.

Paul Hills talked about working with people with more enthusiasm than experience . . .

That's the gamble you take at the beginning. Your potential crew are not that experienced, but you have an idea that they might be good at their job. That's how you can make the film for the money you have. Then in a year's time, everyone is trying to get hold of your by now 'experienced' crew.

So a producer has to gamble on being able to select well and co-ordinate people's enthusiasm into the right kind of energy?

Yeah, that's true. When we were trying to pitch *The Young Poisoner's Handbook* we got turned down at the treatment stage by two television companies. I didn't want to go back to them because I felt I couldn't afford to lose my energy. It's complicated to explain. But I didn't want Ben, the director, to get depressed and I didn't want to get depressed. So I decided we'd forget about them. You need morale to keep going. If you get turned down seven times in a row you're going to start wondering whether it's ever going to happen.

Do you think there are a lot of people who could be good film-makers, but because of a certain attitude in the UK towards things like film-making, they never get involved?

Yes I do. The industry here is very southern based. Most people I know who work in it were born in London. So much is based on who you know in this area. I think there could be lots of good producers and directors in other areas of the country who never think about it. They never even dream that they might be able to do it, because they don't come from the middle-class background that most people who end up being producers or directors come from. I doubt that many producers are people who don't have a family or somebody they can go and stay with when they're trying to find money in the early days, or are living off the dole. The people here are middle class and that's something I think should be addressed. People say that if you're really pushy you'll come to the top and you'll do it anyway. What if you haven't even thought about doing it? The British film industry is only as good as its ideas and energy. But half of it is made up of people whose ambition is to be seen in the right place with the right people. They act as if they were in LA, but we don't have the Hollywood machine to sustain it.

Caleb Lindsay

'If you keep thinking about it, you'll never do it. So it's a case of just doing it.'

Caleb Lindsay wrote, produced and directed *Chasing Dreams*, his first feature film, about young men trying to hustle a living in today's urban Britain. He was born in London in 1972, and, as he tells us in this interview, took his first steps into film around the age of twelve. He went straight from making pop promos to a feature, heeding advice that there is only a very small market for shorts. One of the ways he kept the costs of *Chasing Dreams* down was by avoiding the use of artificial light and shooting on fast film. He has made a further feature, *Contact*, and is going on to make another, *Hard Edge*, both shot on 35mm CinemaScope.

I started at about the age of twelve, messing around with Super 8 cameras doing little stop-animation films. That progressed into trying to tell stories. I couldn't cut the stuff I had shot because I had no machinery, so I had to cut it within the camera. From there I took a massive tangent and went into music for a few years. The good thing about that was it led me to bands, and everyone wanted to make videos.

So I started going into promos, which is my main grounding. I shot about fourteen promos before I made my film. The bands had literally no money. You have to learn all the skills as best you can because you can't afford to hire anyone: you have to edit the thing yourself, you have to direct it yourself. You have to do all the jobs. I started doing promos when I was about seventeen. I think four of them played on MTV. They went on to the independent slot, which showed I could do it, so I got more work.

Did you make shorts first or did you go straight to making a feature film?

Straight to a feature. I thought I was going to make a short. But everyone told me there was absolutely no point in making a short. You can't sell a short. So my initial idea was to make a feature on the same kind of money that you would make a short on. That was my objective, there's much more power in a feature. Loads of people make shorts.

How many people worked on it?

Me, I had someone to light for me. The crew was four people.

So the lighting person shot it?

I did, I operated.

Will you continue to do that?

For the next film I'm going to try and get an operator. I want a monitor so I can show everyone what the shot's all about. But if I can't afford that equipment then I'll operate. One of the things that I found when I was making the film and was surrounded by film students – this isn't a reflection on all film students – was that they had all these great ideas for films and they'd give me their breakdown or tell me what their film was about and it was always epic shots. Then they'd say, 'I'll make it in two years from now, because then the time should be right.' My feeling is that the time is never, ever right. If you keep thinking about it you'll never do it. So it's a case of just doing it. Some of these people were older than me, twenty-eight or whatever. When is it going to happen? They think: 'If I go and get a price on stock I'll probably fall down in shock.' And often that's where it stops: 'I can't do it.' They always want to be told they can't afford to do it.

Paul Brooks was saying his best advice to people who want to make films is to set a date and do it.

Good advice, but you do need money. At the end of the day you'll have learnt something, you'll have made a film and at least you tried. A lot of my motivation was meeting people who talked about doing it but never did it. I really don't want to be one of these people who say they're going to make a film but never do, because you make yourself look like an idiot and you feel like an idiot.

What were your main problems shooting Chasing Dreams?

Mainly a lack of money and time. Because we were doing all the locations on the fly we'd often get kicked off and we'd have to reorganise a scene. For example, we were shooting at a hospital and it was supposed to be a normal ward but we ended up in a children's ward. They were going to kick us out, they didn't even know we were meant to be there. It was supposed to be arranged. So I rewrote the scene with the actors trying to accommodate the fact that there were teddy bears all around and elephants on the wall.

Towards the end of the film I was running out of stock so I couldn't cover scenes quite the way I wanted to. It's very difficult when you can't do a whole close-up of the whole scene, and you don't really know what you need until you start cutting the stuff. That's when you suddenly discover in the spot close-up that someone's moved. Normally when you go into a close-up you go through a whole scene from the beginning on that actor. A spot close-up means that, rather than doing the whole scene in close-up, you're just going for certain lines to save stock.

Someone who'd worked for Roger Corman said that he made them shoot in the order of the lighting set-ups. So that the lights would only be set up each way once, rather than going back and forth.

I didn't use lights. I hate lights with a vengeance, so I shot the whole film on 200 ASA. All the night stuff on the streets and in Kentucky Fried Chicken were shot without them. The problems came with the lighting cameraman. He said, 'You need lights, it's all going to go green.' It doesn't go green. Even if it does go slightly green, the lab when they grade it can pull the green out.

How did you know that?

A calculated guess. If they can grade blue out, which I've seen, then they must be able to take green out. It saves so much time. If I'm trying to shoot in Kentucky Fried Chicken it'll probably take a lighting cameraman eight hours to light the shot. I get the scene together, I put the camera up, I'm just using available light. It happens there and then. Anyway I prefer available light because it looks the way it's meant to look. The best lighting cameramen are lighting cameramen who don't use much light.

When it comes to directing actors and all that kind of stuff, I think it's more of a case of casting the right kind of people. I don't like the directing ethos when they tell an actor what to do to the finest detail. Any input they might be able to bring to it, any kind of life, is just being drained out of it. In *Chasing Dreams* I didn't let that happen, I didn't want that to happen and I'll never let that happen. I want some form of energy to come out of people. That's what makes it interesting.

Stefan Schwartz

'I still don't understand how a film is financed.
Basically, they're made on relationships.'

Stefan Schwartz founded the Gruber Brothers with Richard
Holmes. He directed and wrote *Bonded* and *The Lake*, two
half-hour films, and went on to direct *Soft Top, Hard Shoulder*,
a feature comedy written by Peter Capaldi. It won the 1992
London International Film Festival and two Scottish BAFTA
awards, for best film and best actor. It was also nominated for
an Ivor Novello Award for best soundtrack. World rights have
been sold through Mayfair International. He has recently completed *Giving Tongue*, a BBC Screen 2 feature film starring
Charlotte Coleman, Clare Holman, Clive Francis, Jane
Lapotaire and Peter Capaldi. In this interview he suggests that
because Britain has never built up a star system, the British
feature film industry lacks the fuel to drive it forward and
people consequently gravitate towards the US where serious
money is put into film.

You write your first film thinking you're going to make it. But I certainly
didn't make the first one I wrote. Most directors don't make the first film
they write, but they don't let that put them off. I set out to make this first
film, couldn't make it, wrote another one, couldn't make that. I just kept
writing films, trying to make them. *Soft Top, Hard Shoulder* was a film that
Peter had written. I felt that it had a kind of charm and a lead character
you could like in spite of yourself. We just started developing it with no
real aim in sight, no time scale, just casually.

We had our hands in three other films, two finished scripts and a third
that we were writing. I was also making short films. Each time I've made
a short film, my career has progressed in leaps and bounds. The first
short film I did Roland Joffé saw. He commissioned a feature, which was
very encouraging. The second film I made, called *The Lake*, was seen by
a wealthy man. He had seen the rough cut and hated it, but then saw the
final cut and loved it, and decided to put some money into a film. The
amount he put in meant the only film we could do was *Soft Top, Hard*

Shoulder. We had the two other films ready as well, but they were much more expensive. So it had to be the script that could be done for the money.

There was no precedent, no one else had made a film for that little money. We asked ourselves what the bare minimum was that we could get away with to be fair to everyone. What could they pay their mortgages on?

Where did you shoot it?

We shot it right across Britain: starting in London, we went up to the Lake District, then up into Glasgow.

How did you deal with the logistics?

I had a chat with Beeban Kidron before I started. I asked her what would be the main thing she would have done differently with *Vroom*, her first film. She said that although she had all these beautiful locations, she spent too much time travelling from one to the next. So when she got there she had two minutes to set up and shoot. She was rushed all the time. I was determined to avoid that so I chose to use just three bases: a base in London, a base in the Lake District and one in Glasgow. All the locations were found close to these bases.

Catering is obviously important.

On a low-budget film, the temptation is to give people stodge. It's cheap and it fills people up. But it makes everyone feel lethargic. If you give them healthy, tasty food, people are happier.

How did it break down between you and the producer?

I had done the shorts with Richard [Holmes] and worked with him for nine years. I knew that I didn't want to be involved in any of the organisational nitty-gritty. I wanted to be thinking about what I was doing in terms of the cast and the look of the thing. I think it's desperately important to just keep concentrating on your job, keep hold of the script. It divided up in quite a traditional sense. Except that Richard's very creative and involved in the script. So if I wasn't sure if a scene worked, I'd have him watch it through.

Before the film was shot I imagine you were involved in getting it all off the ground. To what extent did you have to make things happen?

With the shorts I was far more instrumental in making them happen. You're selling the script, you're getting people involved, talking about it.

With the feature one guy put up all the money, and Richard dealt with him.

Had everybody worked in film before?

No. Everyone had worked in drama before. Quite a few of them had worked in film. But we were stretching people. We had an art director who became a designer; the grip was operating the camera. The cast had a brilliant attitude. They were really behind the project. We got some friends of Peter Collins', and some friends of mine. It's always hard for a new cast member joining a film for a short period of time. So it was my and Peter's and Elaine Collins' job to make them feel welcome, make them feel they were a part of the film, even if they were only there for a day. I think that makes it a happier shoot. The crew knew we wanted to get that feeling, everyone was very nice to them. It makes the performance better if they're comfortable, they relax into it more.

It's a long process, getting a film out, from conception to release. Could you talk about that period of time?

I'd been trying to get features made for eight or nine years. I had times when a film was just about to go and a crucial element wasn't in place and it didn't happen. You get depressed. I ended up not trusting what anyone said until it actually happened. Nothing against the people. A lot of them are trustworthy. But a lot aren't and a lot of them don't follow through. You get hardened to it. So when this guy said he was going to give us the money, we didn't believe him. We were like, 'Maybe he will, maybe he won't.' Because there'd been so many times before. So we weren't particularly excited. It was only when a month or two months later he produced the cheque that we believed it. There it was, and it was happening. It was incredibly exciting.

Then we started thinking of all the elements that had to go into place. Finding a crew you liked, who'd work for the money. Working out design ideas, how it would look, what the feel would be. Suddenly the script is happening and you want to polish it and keep changing bits and pieces. You're desperately excited and you're also incredibly nervous. You've got to balance it all, there are so many elements. You're thinking all the time. The closer you get the more you're working. Initially it's meetings and chatting over ideas. Then, as it gets closer, you're having to pin down specifics. When you're shooting you're so involved you dream about the shots for the next day.

Did you think about it all the time? Or were there times when you liked to watch a movie or escape into something unrelated?

I always go and see films. I always try and spend a bit of time not thinking about my work, going to see friends or hanging out. I work hard, then stop thinking about it. Even so, when I'm sitting on the tube or something, I can be thinking about it. But in the evening I'll often just be tired and not want to think about it at all.

People who find their true joy in making the film rather than having made it, tend to be more absorbed, to need less escape.

It's a balance. When you're concentrating on a film, there's only a certain amount of energy you can put in without going loopy. I have to keep perspective, I have to come away from it in order that I can come back fresh. If I'm totally immersed, I lose sight of things, I miss things. Whereas if I can come away ... I love each of the stages. I love when I'm in pre-production. Like the process I'm going through now, the thought that this piece of writing is going to be turned into drama. And I'm looking forward to the shoot. I love the editing and getting involved with the publicity. Because all the stages are so different, when I finished *Soft Top* I was ready to write again. I was really tired and I wanted to sit down and write for six months. And now I'm ready to get on set again.

How much better do you understand the process now, having made a feature film?

I still don't understand how a film is financed. Basically, they're made on relationships. Relationships that you have and what those relationships kick in. That seems to be the key. If you have a friend who finances films, your film is more likely to be read. Obviously it goes on reputation. If you do a good film, you'll be more likely to get the next one. As a director you're always looking for people who will finance your films and then leave you to get on with them.

I feel I know what I'm doing a bit more. I've got my priorities. The script is definitely at the top. Then the actors are an absolute priority when I'm shooting. I care about what they're doing, I care about what they're feeling, care that they know what they're doing. I think I'll always try to put the actors above everything else. To me, the actors communicate the story. And then cinematography, design, special effects in no particular order. Those are the other elements that are important. But I spend a lot of time with them in pre-production. Then when we're shooting, I hope they just get on with it.

What were your hopes for the film?

We were hoping to get in one cinema for a week. We got a thirty-print release. It was around for a couple of months, so it went way beyond our expectations. We were absolutely thrilled, seeing it do well, winning a couple of BAFTAs and being shown at the London Film Festival. It went to other festivals and was pick of the festival in quite a few.

Did you go to a distributor with the finished film?

We went to them before we made it. They got involved, they said they'd distribute it and were incredibly supportive. They were brilliant to work with and told us what was happening all the time.

That's interesting. The producers of Welcome II the Terrordome [*Simon Onwurah*] *and even* Shopping [*Jeremy Bolt*] *said they didn't know what was happening with distribution. Jeremy Bolt said you know about 5 per cent and you never find out much more.*

We were totally involved in every stage – the posters, advertising. Every element.

Who was the distributor? Are they particularly interested in independent films?

The Feature Film Company. I guess they are. They're a relatively new company. *Soft Top* was probably their first release. No, that's not fair, but it was probably their first big one. I think they just cared about it. They're not particularly well-backed financially, they don't have masses of money to throw into a project. But they structured it very carefully.

Did you promote it a lot?

I let Peter promote the film, because he's a known face and talks very well. Frankly, he's more of a sell than I am.

What is it like, having completed a feature?

Obviously you're very proud. But you realise very quickly that that's all you've done, made one film. I don't have a big track record.

What's the main myth you've had to overcome?

That you come off a film feeling that your next film will certainly be financed. That's a myth. You have to go through the same process, except you're aiming a bit higher. People are a little more interested in you, but basically it's just as hard. Unless your film is a massive success, the next one is just as hard. Well, not quite as hard. Companies who finance films take you more seriously.

What do you think of the independent scene?

I don't agree with low-budget features when some people are getting paid and some not; some people being used because they will work for less money; others being paid because they won't. But if they're on an even deal, all up front, no deviousness going on, I think they're a good thing. They give valuable experience to heads of departments and creative teams, directors, producers, writers. They also give exposure to the cast, putting actors in feature films. What it creates is a bunch of people who want to make bigger-budget films. But there's no real finance in the UK.

Although the BBC are getting behind independent production and Channel Four have been behind it for a while, they aren't getting behind features of any size to make an impact on the market. They're not getting behind $10 or 20 million projects. The projects that, when they work, really pull in big money. Therefore film-makers will always gravitate to the States where serious money is put into film, where film is thought of as a serious industry, with serious money-making potential.

A good thing about the industry we've got is that it's encouraging writers to write for film. For a long time writers in the UK have only been able to earn money writing for TV. We weren't really nurturing the writing talent for features. And you need good-quality material.

And actors suitable for those roles . . .

TV has a stranglehold on production in the UK. We make great TV, the rest of the world says. That gives actors a steady income and interesting parts to play. But it doesn't particularly make stars. Whereas feature films do, and they give a different status to actors. But we can't afford to have stars here. Not in a British feature, unless it's funded by the States. We will never really build up a star system. A star system is what fuels a feature industry. If you have a lot of stars who want to work in your country, you can guarantee a certain level of interest in the films they're in. We don't have that so we will constantly lose our talent to the States. Until serious money is put into and made out of films produced here, I can't see the film industry turning around in a big way. Every once in a while we'll come out with a hit like *Four Weddings and a Funeral* that does incredibly well.

What about film-makers not caring too much about money, just a place to sleep and food to eat?

That's all well and good. But once you've made that first film and you've fought for it and you've said 'I don't care about money', then the next one you think: 'Well, I care a little more about it. Because I've been living like shit for ten years and would like to get a bit of money on this next one.' Then the one after that you think: 'I'm experienced now, I've got something to offer, I should get paid for it.'

The first film isn't really about money; it's about making the film and coming out with it. Then you start thinking that you want to get paid. You'll still compromise on money, but you do want to get paid. You want to feel it's sustainable. Otherwise you'll have to get a job elsewhere, because you're not going to be able to live.

Once films make more money, the City will recognise it as a viable investment opportunity ...

Perhaps. But there's no real tradition for Britain to invest in films. Not recently anyway. I think British film-makers have a lot to offer, so here's hoping.

Simon Onwurah

'The costs can always be made to outweigh any profit made.'

Simon Onwurah went to Central Saint Martin's School of Art, London, where he studied film and video. He went on to produce *Welcome II the Terrordome*, a feature film funded by small investors and individuals. The film took several years to complete and threw up all sorts of problems from continuity to tracking down crew and cast members to reappear months later. The advance from the distributor is likely to be the only money the film-makers see in such a film. Simon Onwurah works mainly in television and has just finished *Benin Tales*, a half-hour docudrama for the BBC. He gave this interview shortly after the opening of *Welcome II the Terrordome* in the UK.

Terrordome started life as a National Film School project by Ngozi Onwurah, the director. It was going to be a twenty-minute piece of images set to rap music. That was the original concept. Once we had done that we thought about extending it slightly to incorporate a story, so we extended it to fifty minutes. After that Ngozi wrote the script and we decided to take the big step and make it into a feature.

How much money did you spend?

The total budget in terms of money spent was $300,000. I can't remember how it broke down. The last one we did, particularly the post-production, was quite expensive.

How did you raise the money?

It was an elaborate thing. Family and friends at first, and then we decided to come up with a private investors' scheme which tapped small investors, individuals. Some money came from sponsorship by companies as well. So individuals, business, family and friends, and then in the last stages Channel Four came in to help with post-production.

When you started the fifty-minute thing how many extra people did you bring in?

That was when it changed from being a National Film School film to being a company film. We brought in a whole group of other people who were working with the production company. They started to work on the film. The production company had to do other things to generate money. We were doing other films at the same time as trying to raise money for *Terrordome*. You can only do a *Terrordome* once in your life, or a film like *Terrordome*. It was painful, you know. A lot of the time we were taking big chances, risks, scrambling around to get money, planning the logistics like rounding up everybody to shoot again. Continuity was a nightmare – the children aged from nine to thirteen. There were so many logistical problems. So I would never do a *Terrordome* again, but it was the only way we could have made a feature like *Terrordome*, because there was no way we could get funding on a script like it. Ngozi has said she felt she didn't have the usual editorial constraints that you do when you work on industry productions, but then that was compromised by the fact that she didn't have the money so she couldn't shoot scenes she wanted to shoot.

I heard there were continuity discrepancies in the clothing style, that five years ago the style was to wear trouser ends turned up, and now it isn't.

Also the style of dancing. Some of the dance scenes we did were some of the earliest scenes. That's when we were doing it all to music, so some of the dance is very dated. I mean some of the guys are doing the Running Man. It's amazing, though, how it gels as a film. I mean I spot loads of things like different ways the bandannas have been tied. You've got to remember, we tied one bandanna four years ago and the last bandanna was tied six months ago. No one has really commented on the continuity but we know the problems that went into trying to keep the continuity reasonable. Like I said the children grew in height. Between nine and thirteen is when you sprout and so we had to keep measuring and putting the adult actors on blocks so the height relationship was still the same. The whole thing takes so long when you're doing an independent film, unless it's all secured up front and that's obviously what you have to aim for, secure as much as you can up front. The thing about British cinema is that it's reluctant to take risks. It's very parochial, the themes are quite specifically English, about Englishness or Britishness, whereas cinema is about universal themes. That's part of trying to make *Terrordome* cinematic, trying to really give it cinematic life. Some British films are good but often very like television.

I understand you got through a number of co-producers?

There were different producers at different stages. There was one woman whom I worked with in the early stages, and then doing the later blocks I worked with two other guys. I mean, you need teamwork to try and raise money and crew and motivate people.

I suppose people lost faith sometimes. It's hard enough to keep deferred-payment people working for a year, let alone five.

Exactly. That's what I'm saying about motivation, especially when you've shot and then you pause or stop, it's difficult to get people to come back. The second time they may come back, the third time obviously they want to move on, so you have to motivate them to get them back. So we did go through different crews. I mean, the core crew stayed the same – we had the same lighting cameraman, we had the same designer and the same editor – but on the periphery we went through lots of different crews.

What did it feel like to finally get it out?

For us the film was totally finished in about July, so between July and January when it was released we obviously did other things while the distributors handled when it was going to be released, the advertising campaign and so on. So we've moved on from *Terrordome* to a large extent. Finally finishing it and putting it down after all that time was about eight months ago, so that numbed slightly the effect of getting it out there but obviously we're happy. It's the biggest satisfaction, that we have actually managed to get it out there.

Was Friday the premiere or was there a premiere before that?

Well we've had a number of screenings. Friday was the first screening for the general public, but we've had premieres, festival screenings, cast and crew screenings, industry screenings . . .

Can you tell me about Metro Tartan. How were they with you and what advice would you give people dealing with them and dealing with distribution in general?

Terrordome was a brilliant learning curve in terms of the later stages of production. Normally the productions I'd worked on have been TV oriented; cinema delivery requirements were a lot different, the quality has to be a lot higher. Metro Tartan are an interesting company and in terms of distributors they are one of the best for new and non-A-list films – that's their core market, they don't particularly deal with big films, but they do them well all the same in terms of marketing. They came in quite early. I've been working with them for about a year now and I've got no real complaints about them. With all distributors, you have to remember where they're coming from. You need to make sure that you get money up front from them. If a distributor tells you, for example, that whatever the film makes in the cinema they'll give you whatever, do a split with you, something vague like that, remember that the only real way the production company or the director are going to see money on that is if the distributors give you an advance: once the money is in their account system, creative accountants can be hired quite easily so as to make it very hard to prove that a film has made money at the box-office – the costs can always be made to outweigh any profits made. Get an advance from them and then just work with them to market the film. They will come with their own ideas – they think that they're more experienced at that side of things and that the production company are just good at doing stories – but when it comes to marketing they may become too precious. Work with them, tell them you want to be consulted.

So what were your delivery requirements?

You've got loads of delivery requirements [*laughter*]. Your main delivery requirement is obviously a 35mm print for cinema. It depends what you're shooting on but 35mm and a show print are basic. All along you're using the negative, then you make a print. Your dub has to be stereo, you've got to deliver them different tracks, M&E [music and effect] tracks, loads of stills, loads of music cue sheets. The delivery requirements are extensive.

A trailer?

They may insist, it depends, you can negotiate that; we actually negotiated that out, because we couldn't afford to do a trailer, so they had to do a trailer. But a lot of distributors will insist on the company doing the trailer.

Wouldn't they want to do it themselves?

A lot of times you deliver them a trailer and then they might make changes to it, but you deliver the initial thing. You can negotiate that out if you just can't afford it. Just say, 'Look, you have to do it, we haven't got the money!'

Can you tell me what it was like on set?

A set is a very crazy place if you've never been on one, with quite a few people, lots of people, all doing different jobs. Sometimes people who walk on set think that it's a place where a lot of people just stand around. This isn't true. It's just that in order to set up a shot people have to work very hard, but when you're actually shooting there are not many people actually working. They've done their work and then you finish the shot and then they do their work again. So it can be quite a daunting place, but once you have knowledge of what's going on it becomes a very exciting place. It really is hard work. Everything's got to be done as quickly as possible because time is money in film and if you're doing big sets – and a lot of the time on *Terrordome* we were, even though we didn't have much money – with lots of extras and a great deal of very difficult co-ordination to do, people have to be really on the ball and know what they're doing. We were also dealing with a lot of kids and there are laws in terms of how you can work them and what sort of things you can do with them, so all the logistics have to be very tight. We were doing a lot of night shooting and you build up quite a bond among the crew. Obviously there are different personalities, different egos – a lot of people who get involved in film have big egos, that's part of what attracts them to it, it's a way that they can express themselves – so there can be conflict, but as long as people know that the whole unit is working together then you can get a really good spirit among the crew. I think it's a good idea if people who want to get into film go down and observe a set. If you know anyone who's filming just observe and then during lunch breaks or whatever just ask people what they're doing and why they're doing it. Then you start acquiring knowledge and as soon as you acquire knowledge you're in a better position.

Are there any particular stories?

We were shooting off a lot of guns throughout the filming of *Terrordome* and sometimes the police would come down and ask what was going on. One time an irate resident set his dogs on us and threatened a number of people, even though we'd told everyone around that we were filming and what we'd be doing. You have to be calm in that sort of situation. I remember once we went on location, taking the whole crew – about fifty people – up to Wales to do some underwater sequences, and it rained constantly. It was meant to be sunny Africa and it rained constantly, and we were just about to turn back and we were really getting depressed because we were spending all this money and the weather wasn't clearing. And then someone went to the local village and got this local who was a rain dancer and he did a dance for us and the rain actually stopped!

Bill Britten

'There's nothing you can do with good actors, a great director, a brilliant art director, a fantastic cinematographer, and a bad script.'

Bill Britten grew up in Surrey. He read psychology at Oxford University, then studied acting at the Central School of Speech and Drama. After that he worked as an actor in theatre and TV. He wrote, produced, directed and edited a 25-minute drama on video before going on to make *One Night Stand*, a short shot on 35mm. It was shown in several cinemas and nominated for a BAFTA in 1994. He is now attached as a director to BBC Screen One and has been working as director and co-writer for an independent feature film in development. He suggests that if there were more good shorts being shown, people would come in to see the short and then sit through the commercials before the main film.

We could have had it in as many cinemas as we could have supplied prints for. The Curzon, MGM and Odeon groups all offered to run it. The Curzon offered to pay forty pounds a week, the other two nothing. All three were genuinely wanting to help, but didn't feel they could justify paying out money. Or, in the case of the Curzon, felt that only a token payment was appropriate. But it's a glossy, pacy, Hollywood-style movie and I felt that to put it in an art-house cinema in Mayfair was just not the right place. MGM offered to run it with *Decadence*, the Steven Berkoff film. Again, my feeling was that that was not the right kind of film for it to be with. The Odeon offered to run it with *Malice*, which was exactly right. I think they would have run as many prints as we could have provided. So we got five prints in all. I paid for one myself, two of the film's sponsors paid for the others. The lab let us have the final graded print, which was almost as good as the showprint, free.

So, no distributor?

No. There's nothing in it for them. Well, I think there is something in it for them in that the punters come out feeling they've had something for nothing. It all contributes to their feeling of a good evening's entertainment. Also, if there were shorts running before the commercials, more people would come in to see the short and would then sit through the commercials. I know a lot of people who ring the cinema and ask when the film starts because they don't want to sit through the ads. Whereas, if they knew there was going to be a reasonable short beforehand, they might come in.

In the past shorts were funded through the Eady Levy. This was a tax on cinema tickets. The money raised went back into production. Thatcher abolished that along with just about everything else. The thing about that was, if you made a dreadful short film, but you got it playing alongside, say, *ET*, you would make shitloads of money. You got a proportion of the box-office. People don't go and see films because of the short, they go and see the movie they want to see. Companies were making rubbishy cheap shorts, just to collect their share of the Eady Levy. Therefore short films got a very bad reputation. They are difficult to make and they are usually people's first films.

Why are shorts difficult to make?

Just because making a film is difficult and usually shorts are people's first go at it. They're usually much, much too long. I've hardly seen any short films which aren't too long. *One Night Stand* is twelve minutes. I was very conscious of that. I think someone else telling the same story would have made it twenty minutes. The only thing I'd done before that was a piece on video, which was much too long. That's where I learnt that less is more. It's not just in the shooting, it's in the editing as well. It really is cut cut cut, because people pick things up very quickly. I've seen a number of shorts recently where at the beginning there are five minutes of credits and finally it comes proudly to the bit where it says a so-and-so production and a such-and-such film. You can do that in a feature film because you're prepping people for two hours of sitting there, but not for a short. Just get on with it! Also the longer it is, the less likely you are to get it in the cinema, because the exhibitor has to find a feature film which is under two hours.

You think people who make short films can and should try and get them shown in the cinema?

I'm not sure, because I think it's been changing month by month. When I did it in early 1994 they were really helpful and really encouraging. My understanding is that the exhibitors are much more willing to help than they were several years ago, but it'll cost you money. In the end *One Night Stand* was shown in Kensington, Guildford, Bristol, Manchester and Newcastle. They were the places I asked for, because they were where a lot of my investors were from and I wanted it to be in a cinema near them. We didn't get Leicester Square because of the Christmas break. But Mike Archibald, who was the guy at the Odeon I was dealing with, would have had it, if he could have. I would have liked to have been in Leicester Square.

It depends on what the function of the film is, what the objective is. What is the objective of getting the film in the cinema? Is it glory? Which is fine, I'm not knocking it, but you're not going to make any money. It's going to cost you money to put it in the cinema. You can argue that it'll have a higher profile and you'll be more likely to be able to sell it subsequently. That certainly is the case for feature films. I'm not sure that it works for shorts. The television companies have got you by the short and curlies anyway, they'll pay what they'll pay. They don't care whether it's been in the cinema or not. But a cinema showing raises your profile. One of the reasons you're here interviewing me rather than somebody else who made a short film is because I had a cinema release. If you have a profile, you're more likely to get a feature film to do. A cinema release does help that.

How many showings were you at? It must be good to feel the audience's reaction.

That's why I went to one. Unfortunately there were only about thirty people there. I didn't feel I could ask the cinema for repeated free tickets because the manager of the cinema wasn't particularly friendly. I think she felt she'd had it foisted on her by people further up. There's a limit anyway to how much time you want to spend watching your film when you've already seen it 250 times. I'd done that already with festivals. I've been to quite a few festivals where it was showing: London, Dublin, Cannes – Cannes was a good one – and Emden in Germany. It was also shown at Stockholm and it won a couple of awards at French festivals in Angers and Brest. Also Rio, Seattle, Sainte Thérèse in Canada, Leeds, Southampton.

Ray Brady, director of Boy Meets Girl, *a film that had a lot of problems with the BBFC, says that taking a film around to a lot of festivals and getting a lot of press gave his film a higher profile.*

In any kind of film-making publicity is important. At festivals you meet people, not only from abroad, but other British people who are doing the same thing. Several people said to me that when you go to Cannes don't hang out with the Brits, try and meet the people you won't see the rest of the year, who you can't get access to because they're not in London. I did all that and frankly I think I'd have been better off spending my time with the Brits because you get access, at places like Cannes, to the people who make the decisions in this country. It's just contacts. It's impossible to assess exactly what it's worth but I think it's quite valuable. I've only been to three or four festivals. I happen to be very broke because I spent all my money on making a film.

How much did One Night Stand *cost?*

The budget was £21,000. It cost £18,000 to make with £3,000 spent on prints and marketing. Then after that I spent at least another £2,000 in bits and pieces just picking up bills for various things. This wasn't in the budget proper but came out of my pocket.

Was it deferred payment or was it no payment at all?

Well, I haven't used the phrase 'deferred payment' at all. I don't want to bullshit people. There was never any way that they were going to get paid anything, they all knew that. I specifically said to several of the key people, 'Why do you want to do this?' If you've got somebody working on your film who doesn't have a good reason to, they're going to let you down. I also remember reading a piece of advice from an American, who said to shoot on 35mm. He said that if you shoot on 16mm you will find that on day three your cameraman rings in to say he's got flu and your script supervisor doesn't turn up because she can't find a babysitter. If you're shooting on 35mm your cameraman will be mainlining analgesic to keep standing upright and your script supervisor will be ringing people in Bosnia to try and find a babysitter. It looks a lot better too, and it's got snob value.

You have aspirations to do a feature soon. How is it going?

I don't know about soon, but I'm working it! I'm not a very good writer. The hardest thing is finding a good writer. Everybody is looking for good scripts. Absolutely everybody. There are a lot of writers starting out saying, 'Nobody will take me seriously, nobody will read my script. I've got this wonderful script and I can't get it made.' The brutal truth is that it is probably because it's not a very good script. I spent most of the last year looking for a good writer. Not just a good script, but somebody I think I can work with, who has got what it takes. It's very, very hard to find people who can write cinema. There are a lot of people writing quite passable TV. But there is a big difference between writing cinema and writing TV. There are a couple of writers I've come across whose work I like. We're trying to find the right project and kicking ideas backwards and forwards. You've got to find a writer, then you've got to find the idea. That is the single biggest problem. There's nothing you can do with good actors, a great director, a brilliant art director, a fantastic cinematographer, and a bad script.

A lot of it depends on what sort of movies you're talking about. The kind of movies I want to make are *movies*, not films like European art house. A lot of my favourite films are European art-house films, but they're not what I think I can do. In European art-house films direction, acting and look are possibly more important. You can crudely split films into those which are entertainment and those which are art. In entertainment it's only really the script that counts. If it's a good story well put together, it only needs to be passably acted and passably directed. There are so many quotes. Hitchcock said, 'There are three things that count, the script, the script and the script.' Somebody else said that if you get the script right, you can phone in the direction. Any idiot can do the direction if you get the script right. Frankly I agree with that. That's the director's chief skill, getting the script right. It's not necessarily right when the writer says it's right. That's also part of the producer's skill. It's not just taking the script you're given and making it. That's where a lot of TV goes wrong.

So you'll wait for the right time to do a feature.

I want to make a feature tomorrow. But it's a question of getting the *right* script. There are several I've got already. There's a fully finished script by one of these two writers that I've come across. This guy is very good. It's a European art-house film actually, but it's a beautifully written script. There is a producer I'm working with who has just started putting it out to the BFI, Channel Four and so on. They may all come running saying, 'Yes, perfect script, let's do it now.' More likely one of them will say, 'Not my sort of thing', and another will say, 'Well maybe if you did this . . .' That's the way it goes. We could go into pre-production almost immediately. I'd need to do another two months' work on the script until I know it backwards. But as a project it's there.

I'm not entirely sure that the way things are going with independent films is healthy. There are a lot of private films made with money from one or two investors. People who don't know anything about film – they've just made a packet somewhere else, making the nozzles on aerosol cans or something – love the idea of making a feature film. They find some likely lads who've got a script and silver tongues and they say, 'You're the experts, here's the money, go make the film.' But these producers don't have anybody behind them to say to the film-makers, 'You're not ready. This script is not ready. You need another rewrite.' That's the function of the usual financing institutions, that's why distributors know their business. I don't mean that they're infallible by any means. But there is another pressure, another layer of . . . if you wanted to knock it you'd call it bureaucracy. Another layer of executive producership. People standing well back from the project saying, 'I haven't read the script for three months, I will now reread it and see whether I think it is ready to shoot.' And they read it and they may say, 'No! That's not right, don't think that character works well. Another rewrite, please.' That's not happened with a lot of these films.

But the only way you learn about films is to make films, surely?

No, I don't think so. People who work in distribution have never made films but, by God, they know what sells.

Do they though? They're sales people so they have to know. But though they can get a nose for what will sell, that may desensitise them to other things, newer ideas that would also sell. You only have to look at the cinema listings to see that there isn't much of a spectrum. Maybe people would go for more of a spectrum. The big distributors usually go for safe bets.

Some of that's true, every now and then they do trip over something and they all kick themselves.

The impression I've got from the interviews so far is that establishment doesn't encourage independent film-makers.

The answers are all in William Goldman's book *Adventures in the Screen Trade*. He says 'nobody knows anything'. Everybody tries to have a rough idea of what will or won't sell. But they don't really know anything. If you haven't read the book, read it. I suspect that the distributors are very canny about what they can sell. Even if it's a crap movie, *The Flintstones* was a crap movie. I don't know anybody who came out of that film saying they enjoyed it. But, by God, millions of people went to see it! It was brilliantly sold. The distributors knew, or at least suspected, that they could sell that film. They live or die by their ability to predict what will or won't sell. I'm not saying they're infallible, but it's risky to remove that layer of people standing back from the project saying, 'We'll only give you the money when we think it's ready to go.' I do know one or two independents who have recently shot mouldy scripts, real dogs, with private money. But they've got the money because the private investors don't know. They love the idea of film. They've got a star or a minor star in it. The producers have convinced them that they're ready; the producers have probably convinced themselves that they're ready. I think we're going to end up with a situation where, if you say, 'It's an independent British film', people are going to say, 'Oh God, no!' That's how I feel. Some of them are very good. But a lot aren't.

Tim Dennison

'You've got to have a good script. You've got to be very happy with the plot line. You've got to work the script until you're 100 per cent happy with it.'

Tim Dennison was educated at Clevedon Comprehensive School and Woking Sixth Form College. He first worked as a runner for a commercials production company in the early 80s. He ran on feature films and started assistant directing on films such as *Wetherby, Personal Services* and *Little Shop of Horrors. Revenge of Billy the Kid* is the first feature he produced and is a comedy horror 'about a farmer who has a torrid liaison with a goat which gives birth to a half-man, half-goat'. He says you have to have some marketing hook for your film if you have no stars and no budget. It's one thing to make the film and another to sell it.

I started in the film industry about twelve years ago as a tea boy and acquired my union ticket. Then I had numerous jobs as an assistant director. Then I met a film editor called Jim Groom and we formed a company called Montage Films. The idea was to find three different scripts with three different budget scales – £1 million, 2.5 million and 5 million – in three different genres.

We then had a stroke of luck with the office we had on lease in Wardour Street. We were approached by a representative of a property company. They told us that they were buying up the building and asked us how much money we wanted to surrender the lease to them. We said fifty grand. So they said, 'Okay we'll give you fifty grand.' We should have held out for more in retrospect, but hindsight is a wonderful thing. With £50,000 we decided to get on with making our first film, which we decided to write.

Myself, Jim Groom and a friend of ours called Ross Smith, who had submitted a script to us called *Sleighride to Hell* went down to the Stockpot. It's a cafe where you can get a proper meal for something like £1.50. We decided what the premise for our first film was going to be, and who should direct, write and produce. When you make your first film and you've got no money, people for some reason always do horror films. *Billy the Kid* was a comedy horror. You have to have some marketing hook, if you have no stars and no budget. We came up with the idea of what would happen if a goat gave birth to a half-man half-goat.

I can't remember exactly how long it took us to write. We did a few drafts over two or three months. When we started shooting the film it was a logistical nightmare. Through our inexperience we totally cocked up the first few days. For example, we hired a seven-and-a-half-ton truck to take all the camera equipment, all the lighting equipment, the costume department, the art department, the office production equipment, everything. So all the necessary facilities were stuck in this one big truck, and by the time the truck had travelled the six hundred miles or whatever it was to the location, they had got lost. Normally you have a truck for each particular department. We had all the departments in one and that was a big mistake.

We over-scheduled or under-scheduled. The first day we were filming until two o'clock in the morning. We didn't allocate enough responsibility to other people. When you've got no money you try and cover everything yourself. By the time we got to Wales after a week of shooting, we were already two days behind schedule. But for the thought of failing, especially of letting down thirty or so people all under the age of twenty-five, I would have given up after the first week. But we managed to get ourselves to Wales and filmed for a month. It was only through the crew's guts and dedication that we managed to continue. So we finished filming. Once the five weeks were over we'd shot about 60 or 70 per cent of the film and blown our fifty grand. We came back to London, cut the footage that we had, and decided to follow up two routes to finish the picture.

We cut a promo reel, about twenty minutes long, and took ourselves down to Cannes with a tent. Thanks to advice from Ross Smith, who'd been to Cannes numerous times before, we took some tuxedos, because we thought that we would have to wear them all the time. So there we were, three young spotty-nosed prunes, walking down the Croisette in their suits, sweating away, carrying their briefcases containing their precious promo reel. People were looking rather shocked, sitting in their hotels drinking their pina coladas in their short-sleeved Hawaiian shirts.

We had some interest from various distribution companies. But they wanted to see a finished product. A lot of distributors were wary of the subject matter. In retrospect we should have been more punchy and had a concept for them. We came back from Cannes demoralised. Then Jim came up with the idea of putting an ad in *Private Eye*: 'Film company seeking £70,000 to finish their comedy horror film *Revenge of Billy the Kid*.' A couple of days later we had a phone call in the evening from a 29-year-old entrepreneur living in Grimsby. We sent him a package with the promo reel and publicity and he agreed to finance the remaining filming.

We managed to recruit most of the original crew and ended up filming for another four or five weeks. We then did a couple of screenings for all the distributors and sales agents from the UK. The publicity that we had on the making of *Billy the Kid* was very good, 100 per cent due to Ross. We were in all the major journals and even appeared in *Film '92*. They were doing a special section on newcomers working on no-budgets.

So distributors knew about us when we eventually screened the film. We had three offers. Through our naiveté we went with the company with the highest profile. However, when we made the agreement with them we thought we'd get a theatrical release. We never did, we were never informed about what was going on.

We also had troubles with our private investor. One of his conditions for putting in money was that we formed a separate company. He controlled that company. So, to a certain extent he controlled the film. It's just one of the many pitfalls of making the bloody thing. When you sell it you get screwed on the distribution.

So, we managed to make *Billy the Kid*. It was arduous and time-consuming and we eventually had to put our company into liquidation. But we had a film under our belt.

After that a few months lapsed while we recovered. Then we wrote another script called *Zombie God Squad*. It's a comedy horror picture about a fictional town called Stockton, which is going to be bought up by an American conglomerate owned by the Devil. The Americans want to get all the residents out of Stockton so they can turn it into a Disneyland for the Devil. We packaged it, scheduled it, budgeted it and approached various people to be in it. Eventually we got Peter Cook to play the lead role. We approached various companies to raise the finance. Again we had problems with the subject matter. We seem to write scripts which are slightly off the wall. When films are hard to get off the ground, you need to know your market and try to minimise the negative sides of your project. People were wary of it.

We approached a company called Metrodome Films for finance. Paul Brooks at Metrodome passed on the subject. But at the time he'd just acquired the film rights to a book called *Bedlam*. He wanted somebody to do the mechanics of putting the picture together. So we agreed to line produce *Beyond Bedlam*. It ended up being called that because of the old RKO picture, *Bedlam*. When you finish a picture, you have to fulfil what are called delivery requirements for your sales agent. One of those requirements is that when you sell your picture to the States no distributor will take your picture unless you have an insurance policy called an E&O (errors and omissions). The Yanks sue over anything. Part of the E&O insurance policy is that you have a title check. There's a company that's called Thomson and Thomson who will scan everything. You get a title report back covering films, books, theatre, TV series, anything like that.

After line producing *Beyond Bedlam* we decided it was time to make our own project again. One day we got Jim's camera equipment out and said, 'Right. We've got the camera equipment here, we've got the editing gear here, we know where the manpower is, let's write a script, build our own set and shoot another film.' We wrote another script called *Room 36*, a black-and-white thriller set in a hotel. We shot the bulk of it over two weeks. Then we did two or three weekends of pickups, primarily exteriors. We shot the film on a ridiculously low amount of money. We just got our friends to put up a few grand each. It was a case of trying to prove to ourselves that it can be done, and to produce something that's a commodity. We shot the film on 16mm and managed to persuade a lab to blow the film up to 35mm. We've screened the film for various distributors. No bites yet. The response from a lot of people has been that the opening was too long. So it's been recut and there will be a fine cut of the new cut next week!

What have you learnt from these experiences?

You've got to think things through. It is very hard to make a film, no matter what the budget is. You have to limit the risks. With *Billy the Kid* we had very little money and we wrote an effects-oriented film. It was time-consuming to film and took us over budget. Your script has got to be reasonably simple. You've also got to think, more importantly, what happens when you've finished the film. It's one thing making the film, it's another selling it.

You'll find that most British no-budget pictures, and American ones too, never see the light of day. They just stay on the shelf because nobody will pick them up. Nobody knows the golden answer, how to make *Four Weddings* or *The Crying Game* or *Shallow Grave*. The most important thing is to get the script right.

When you send your script out, the first thing that distributors or financiers will look at is the last page number. If it's 160 pages, then you've lost them. You want a maximum of 120 pages, ideally 90 pages.

You've got to have a good script. You've got to be very happy with the plot line. You've got to work the script until you're 100 per cent happy with it. The other thing you've got to learn is it's not what you know, it's who you know. That means networking, awful as it is. Contacts. That's it.

Kaprice Kea

'Problems are part of the process.'

Frustrated by the lack of communication and support from film institutions for aspiring young talent, Kaprice formed the Peeping Tom's Club in a Soho bar in July 1993 (the name is a reference to Michael Powell's famous film). Since then hundreds have attended the fortnightly events and formed creative relationships. With an emphasis on an 'open-to-all-policy' and readily available free information, the club has done much to educate and empower the grass-roots film community in London. As a committed film-maker, he has also had to strike out on his own to get his work into production. In 1995 he completed *the hurting*, which was produced by Harry F. Rushton. It is a harrowing but sensitive story of male rape which raises many questions about the nature of sexuality. Kaprice discusses the making of the film.

How did the hurting *come together?*

I suggested an idea to Harry, and he went to some private investors for the money. We cut the red tape. We had formed a working relationship on our short film, *Honeymoon Beyond*, which he financed. The film *the hurting* was a follow-on from the short. It was our second project together, and it worked very well. He let me get on with it, while he handled the business side.

The first person to come on board was Nichola Koratjitis, the film's production manager. I'd met her six months before at a preview theatre, and we became good friends. She is one of those people who you can really rely on. We had wanted to work together, but didn't imagine it was going to happen so soon. We set up an office immediately. When you get money promised it doesn't always arrive just like that. But we wanted to shoot in early summer, so we just got on with the job. I think sometimes you just have to do that. Because if you don't go with it, then that chance will slip. We interviewed potential crew, that sort of thing, and made up the schedule. I wrote the script. We had a first draft ready after two weeks.

We did casting. I spent quite a lot of time getting the right actors together. Pre-production was about two months. At one point we were led to believe the money was arriving, and it didn't. But it did come in time.

You said you shot for two fortnights. How long was the break in the middle?

It was a week. We had a scene which is quite lengthy at the end of the film. This film came together so quickly: we got the money in March, wrote the script and were shooting in May. So casting and crewing up happened very quickly. For the final scene we really needed to probe properly. It also gave the crew a chance to have a break.

How were the crew?

Wonderful. They always are. That's part of the pleasure of making films, the human element.

What were the problems?

Problems are part of the process. You need to remain flexible and accommodate change. Sometimes problems just go out the window when you're making a piece of cinema. For example, you get a script broken down into eight pages on the schedule. To someone looking at that document, everything seems equal, every eighth is the same as every other eighth. As a director, you know what is a priority to capture and what is not so important. I found that I would shoot more of the important material and discard things that were less important. Sometimes everyday objects become significant. In television you might dress a whole room, which might include a telephone. In cinema you might not need any of that, you might just want the telephone for that scene. We shot a ten-minute nuisance call, so the phone in *the hurting* is very important. You know the phone's going to be projected across the whole screen in a West End cinema. The props aren't being selected to be shown on a small screen, they have to stand out. They have to be right. You need to prioritise what is important for your images and their desired effect.

Did you manage to achieve your vision?

I don't know so much whether this film was inspired by a vision. It was more of an exploration, we follow the choices an individual makes. I'm satisfied that the film distinguishes itself by the choices made. They are unusual, but believable.

How about the future?

There is no divine law that says I have the right to make another feature. I'd love to. But that would take someone with guts and a big heart, like Harry, to take a risk on my material. There are not many around like him in the industry. Men like him can make dreams happen. Isn't that what cinema is really about?

Philippa Braithwaite

'I didn't write a book ... because I couldn't write the really interesting bits. I'd be done for libel.'

Philippa Braithwaite was educated in a convent, then at sixth form college. After that she attended the London College of Printing where she took a Higher National Diploma in media studies. She had been a producer for about ten years working in television and commercials while looking for a suitable script to turn into a feature. *Staggered* was co-written by her brother and is a comedy starring and directed by Martin Clunes. Like Gary Sinyor and Paul Brooks, she took advantage of the Business Expansion Scheme to finance the movie. As a novice feature producer she found negotiating with agents a problem; both actors' agents and sales agents could have been more helpful. *Staggered* was a commercial success and she is currently developing *Tourist Trap*, a comedy action film which will also be directed by Martin Clunes, and another movie called *Sliding Doors*.

I'm trying to think back to how it all started. I had a talk with my brother who's a scriptwriter. He'd come up with an idea with his co-writer for a film. I thought it sounded great. This was at the end of 1992. I told him to go off and write it and he came back with the script about six weeks later. It was great, a very simple story, a comedy. Just a good idea. We thought, 'Well okay, we'll make it.' I thought, 'How am I going to make it, who do I go to get this film financed?' I thought British Screen would hate it and Channel Four would hate it, because it was just straightforward entertainment with no other pretensions.

This was around the time that *Leon the Pig Farmer* had opened or was about to open. We were watching that quite carefully to see how they did it. It made us think it was possible to do it another way. My brother and I had set up a company together. We went to see the lawyers at a company called Goulden's. They put the finance package together for *Leon the Pig Farmer*. We thought that was the only way we were going to get a film made, to go and get it done off our own backs. We didn't even try sending it off to any of the normal sources of finance. I think if we had, I'd still be here today waiting for replies. I did send it off to one well-known film company and got a letter back exactly a year later on the day the film opened in July 1994 saying, 'Thanks, but we don't think it'll make a very good film.' I thought that just about summed it up. Anyway, we went to see the lawyers. They thought it was a good idea and told us how to package it.

I didn't write a book about how I did it because I couldn't write the really interesting bits. I'd be done for libel. There were a lot of problems. We had to get cast attached, and the agents in this country are pretty unhelpful. Most of them just didn't want to know and put the phone down. It was then that we realised that whatever happened we were going to make the film. It didn't matter how many people or obstacles got put in front of us. We were completely determined to do it.

We used the Business Expansion Scheme. Paul Brooks knows about it, because he was one of the producers on *Leon the Pig Farmer*. It was a brilliant idea, but it's gone now. It was around for about ten years, but *Leon the Pig Farmer* was the first instance of it being used for a film. It involved forming a public limited company and putting together a prospectus. It could be used for anything. A lot of people used it for property deals.

You sell shares in your company to raise money. We put a prospectus together detailing who was going to be in it, who was going to direct it, all to persuade people to buy a piece of the film. We were going to make the film for £150,000. The chances that we would recoup were, I thought, quite high. But there were some really strict financial guidelines you had to follow in drawing the prospectus up. Any producer's natural inclination would be to sell the film by saying it's going to make a lot of money. But film is such a risky thing, the chances are people will not make their money back. You can't make promises you might not be able to keep.

To get shareholders we just rang up absolutely everybody we knew. They'd say 'No', and we'd ask them to give us the number of somebody else who might be interested. Then we got a publicist to publicise the share offer. They got me on the radio, doing press interviews and TV. You had thirty days from the time you launched the prospectus. If you hadn't raised the money in thirty days you couldn't do it. We didn't raise the money in a month, but the lawyer came up with this great legal loophole and managed to extend the deadline another month. In that month we got the rest of the money. That was that. I think we'd got about 130 shareholders and we'd raised about £150,000 pounds.

I was doing a live radio show, and someone asked me what other incentives we were offering. I had the idea that anyone who put in over £500 could be an extra in the film, because we needed to do a big wedding scene with loads of extras. That got us loads of money. It was great because we needed the extras and we couldn't afford to pay them. Getting the money was the hard part. But I knew about production because I'd been working in production for years. Getting the film together wasn't a problem for me.

I got as many really experienced crew people as I could. The crew were brilliant and the production team were brilliant. We still had the problem that we had no money to pay them, which was quite tough. Then again, it was easier in a way than having just a bit of money, because we were saying to people, 'We've got nothing, do you want to do it or not?' So either they did or they didn't. I made sure that everybody liked the script or had read the script from the runners upwards, so that they knew what they were doing and felt part of it.

Martin [Clunes], who directed it, was great. He has amazing energy and gets on really well with everybody, so there was a good atmosphere on set. The shooting of it wasn't really much of a problem.

The one part of it that I didn't know anything about was the distribution and the marketing and the business side. I really threw myself in at the deep end. It was a real shock. I have learnt through baptism-by-fire how it all works, how the different parts of the world you have to sell your film in are divided into territories and how much you should ask each one of them for. I didn't know at the time what the deals were. The sales agent and people didn't rip me off. It was a combination of my naiveté, believing it when they said things like, 'We'll make you this amount of money on this film.' Within three weeks we had recouped the investors' money on paper because we got a big sale from Entertainment who distributed the film.

Now I realise what a lot of sales agents are doing. They just want your film. It really is no skin off their nose because they're not giving you any money up front for it. I've been telling people this about deferred films, but they don't seem to realise the vulnerability of the producer in this situation. People are expecting their money, they see the film doing well, they see its name everywhere and the sales agents are telling the producer that they're going to do this and that. It never comes off. I don't think there is one sales agent in this country who would go to an unknown film-maker and say, 'Alright we'll give you half a million for your film' – or even a hundred thousand. They're not going to do it.

Looking back on it, I would have scrutinised a lot of the deals much more carefully. Or at least checked out the distribution companies we were signing contracts with more carefully. There was, for example, one Korean company we did business with. We were out in Milan for the film market, just after we shot the film, with our promo reel. This company came along and made a contract with us that said they'd give us a hundred thousand for the film. That amount would pay back all my crew. I went back and said, 'We've got this deal that pays everybody back.' In July, six months later, the company just turned around and said, 'No, we're not going to give you the money.'

I said to our sales agent, 'What are we going to do about this? Are you going to sue them?' They told me it wasn't worth their while to try and sue a company based half-way round the world. What it really was, was that they didn't want to jeopardise their relationship with that distributor. There's all this that comes in that you don't realise. Also, if a distributor picks up a film in Korea and registers it, you can't by law then sell it to any other Korean distributor because they've registered it. So we're stitched, we can't sell it there now.

Then a German company who had offered us $200,000 for the film suddenly were being really flaky and weren't coming up with the money. It didn't actually fall through. But they turned around and told us they were going to give us £50,000 less than we'd agreed. I'm still waiting for the rest of it. They've given me some of it. I almost walked away from that because I was so fed up with it. But I had my crew to think of, and my investors. I couldn't walk away from $150,000. It was a risk; I might have got a better deal in Germany.

After we'd made the film, it seemed like the whole process of raising the money and making it was easy compared to the nightmares we've had selling it. Now if I went to a sales agent, I would make sure they gave me money up front. It will be easier because I've made a film that made money, I know what I'm asking for. It's all very well saying, 'Make sure you get money out of them.' But if they won't give it to you, there's not much you can do.

How much did it make at the box-office?

One and a half million. In *Screen International* last week it was number 56 in the top 100, one of only four British films in the top 100. I was really pleased. You have to know your market. I think a lot of people make films here without knowing whom they're making them for. That's why they fall flat on their faces. I know that there's a market of teenagers who go and see films in multiplexes around the country. Not necessarily in London, it did fairly well in London. But it did brilliantly up north, in multiplexes. I always said that it was a multiplex film. Everyone was saying that it wasn't, that it wouldn't do very well. Some of the reviewers liked it, some didn't and said it would do really badly. But it did really well. That makes you feel some kind of satisfaction.

You didn't get a cut out of that one and a half million?

No. I really didn't realise that cinemas took 70 per cent of the take. I knew that the distributors took about 30 per cent and that we take 15 per cent of that 30 per cent. They have to recoup all the costs they spend on the film. We've just broken even with them, even after the video having done so brilliantly. It's been in the top ten since it opened and we won't see a penny out of that, we won't see a penny out of the box-office.

All the way along everybody else is making money. Which would have been fine if we'd all got paid fees for it. But deferred payment was the way we chose to make it. As I said, it was the only way we could make it.

A. Hans Scheirl

'I'm not making a mass product. But you can make the money for more films if you think internationally.'

A. Hans Scheirl was born in Salzburg, Austria. She attended the Academy of Fine Arts in Vienna, where she studied art restoration, and now lives in Vienna and London. She is a filmmaker, performer, writer and artist and is attempting to push forward the boundaries of cinema with her 'no-budget to low-budget films'. In *Dandy Dust* she was aiming for multimedia, cybercomic-splatter-cinema, audiovisual images to see again and again. A few films down the line she hopes to develop a completely new cyber-cinema to 'express the pains, pleasures and transformations of the new era'.

I started by making Super 8 films in Vienna with friends of mine. Like Andy Warhol we called them 'home movies'. We inspired each other, just making films and showing them to friends. They were experimental short films. I didn't do drama; there wasn't any dialogue. Super 8 was so cheap that I didn't even have to write applications for funding. I also didn't want to have to explain what I was doing to any one. I was free to play and teach myself.

It meant that it took a long time; I started to make films in 1979! Eventually I got bored with shorts. You don't have access to proper distribution and I wanted to make cinema. Two friends and I had decided to make a film and that it had to be feature length! I've never really understood Hollywood narrative and had to teach myself to understand narrative and to invent things that way. As a spectator myself I want to be led through, not necessarily in a straightforward line, but I do want to be seduced into following a story. I wrote the script for *Flaming Ears*, for which we got funding from Hamburg and Austria. I make very, very low-budget films. I have an almost socialist way of paying people. On *Dandy Dust*, for example, everyone who worked full time got the same basic fee; enough to pay the rent, really. That's all.

What role were you playing?

The main character was a being with twelve different identities, seven of which were played by me. I was exposing myself very much because it's a very personal film and because it's a sexual film. One minute I'm acting spreading my legs or something. The next I'm the producer and maybe someone has to be fired. It took me a few months to get over that. I mean at the time it was okay because it was so intense. Because I was acting, I could live through the madness.

You said to me earlier that you gave people a lot of breadth, but you were sometimes worried about that.

You can be lucky and you can be unlucky. When the production designer, Mark Harriott, saw the script he said, 'Wow, this is a feast for a production designer because it's so fantastic.' I was so wonderfully surprised with what he came up with that I just let him get on with it. There were little moments when I just thought certain things weren't the way they should be. But I don't regret a bit of it, he's very good.

How much money did you have?

Something between no-budget and low-budget. Low-budget and low-tech belong to the same philosophy of matter. I aim to deal with matter in the language that it speaks, not against the medium but with it, not against limitations but through them. Of course I need a budget. I don't just take some actors and shoot a drama in a warehouse. My films play in artificial worlds. Everything therefore must be made for the film, every set. And there were many. The characters and the extras needed costumes. Working with special effects also slowed down the shoot. *Flaming Ears* was filmed on Super 8, transferred to 16mm and cost about £100,000. *Dandy Dust* will cost more than that, but not much. We hope to have both 16mm and 35mm prints on completion.

How long was your shoot for Dandy Dust?

Eight or nine weeks full time. But of course we weren't shooting all the time, because there were three days of shooting, then one or two days of making a new set.

How many people were there on Dandy Dust? *Were they people you knew or did you advertise for them?*

There were so many people working on it in the summer, I really don't have a figure. The basic set-up was the cinematographer, the camera operator and continuity. One person on lights, sometimes more than that. Then the production manager, then the production designer who had helpers, usually two, sometimes more than that. Ten people helped with models, then costumes, plus make-up people, though we mostly did our

69

own make-up. It was mainly people who I knew or friends of friends. I also put an ad into the National Film Theatre saying I was looking for runners and some other positions. A lot of people reacted to that.

Many of the people I know through the scene, the dyke scene, the club scene, and not just in London. With my last film I was travelling everywhere, to all the gay and lesbian film festivals. That's how I met a lot of people, like Sarah Schulman who writes novels. When she came to London to read at the Institute of Contemporary Arts I met her again and told her I was working on another film. She said that she would like to be in it! People in my films are not actors, they do other things, photographers or philosophers or whatever. I pick them for their performance skills. Some people just have it. There was Trash, from New York, who performs as a male cross-dresser. I like to work with amateurs. Although working with Angela DeCastro, a professional performer who's a clown, was quite a pleasure too.

Did you have a strict shooting ratio?

On video you don't have to worry. On Super 8 you have to be more careful. When we were shooting on 16mm we didn't plan a lot. But that's because the cinematographer Gianna Cipriani is like me, we're both used to working very economically. She is a Super 8 film-maker, like me. With Super 8 you learn to be very economical, very precise and also trust the performers to get it right first time. We also had a precise story board for the whole film to keep it under control.

How long do you think the film will be?

A bit over eighty minutes. I'd rather make a fast and intense film that is not too long. The experience of time in film depends on the kind of storytelling method used. The Japanese film *Tetsuo* is not even seventy minutes, but you really need a rest after seventy minutes!

A lot of amateur films and first films are too long. A lot of films are too long.

That might be because of structural problems in the script. My latest film is full of detail. I showed the script to a professional scriptwriter who told me I couldn't make a film out of it, that there was enough material in it for five films. I was very shocked. But then I have a different kind of storytelling, my films are more like comics. I don't work in a naturalistic way.

It's important to be able to distinguish between good criticism and criticism that doesn't apply to your style of film-making. I suppose you develop that as you go along, and a big part of this is confidence and finding your voice.

You just have to make a few films. I don't think *Dandy Dust* will be my answer. I will be much closer to where I want to get to. But it will take me a few films to develop a new cyber-cinema.

What kind of distribution are you hoping for?

We're still looking for distribution. I'd like it to be distributed somewhere in the Far East, like Hong Kong or Japan.

What about publicity? What do you do when you don't have the advertising budgets to be able to afford big posters on the tube?

Dandy Dust is not just a film, but a mythology and a forum for contemporary cyborgs – people who are living experimental lives, who won't ever take any traditional notions of sex and gender and family and genre for granted again. There is a lot of media attention around drag kings, radical body artists, queer culture. We are creating exposure for each other through photography, books, clubs, performances and so on. We are exhibitionists and know how to create attention. We won't need big posters! I see myself as a cult film-maker, I want to make films that people will want to see again and again. I'm not making a mass product, but you can make the money for more films if you think internationally.

   For instance, I want to make a film in three languages. One character will be talking Japanese or Cantonese and another will be talking German. It will be subtitled. I think that you always have to think how to promote your film, very specifically. There's a very interesting book called *Midnight Movies* about cult films. It talks about the way *Eraserhead* was promoted. *Eraserhead* was a flop at first. It was shown in one cinema in New York and it flopped. Someone looked at it and said, 'Okay, I don't want any advertisements, no posters whatsoever, no press whatsoever, just put this film on every Friday midnight in this one cinema. It has to be a very specific local place.' Then people started to come, and they thought they'd discovered the film. So there are hundreds of ways of doing it. At the moment we are doing trailers, and we really have to raise funds.

What's your impression of independent film-making in Britain at the moment?

The attitude towards innovative film and art in general is appalling here. In Austria there is a much stronger belief in the power of art, in the vital necessity of artistic freedom for the survival of a culture. Here people, even friends of mine, use the word 'arty', as if it was as dirty to do art as it is to show your naked body here. I also find the divisions between 'drama' and other forms of cinema such as genre movies, art-house and pornos limiting. We should get together and proclaim the New Cinema, free from the old boundaries to express the pains, pleasures and transformation of the new era.

71

Steve Simpson

'I've recovered. But I haven't been the same person since.'

Steve Simpson was born and raised in Aberdeen. He left school at seventeen to join a firm of stockbrokers. Two years later he left in order to work in LA for the master of low-budget movies, Roger Corman. Corman's company is so small that he had the chance to work directly for all the different heads of department, including production, distribution and international sales. He returned to Scotland in 1993 to start the production of *Ties*, his first feature film, which he also wrote and directed. He compares making a film to working on the stock markets, finding that the pressure of a hard day working the markets is about 10 per cent of the average pressure you go through making a film. His financial advice to would-be independent film-makers is to reduce the cost of your bills by paying in advance!

I started off making amateur films on video because when I was growing up I loved Bruce Lee and Jackie Chan movies and wanted to choreograph fight scenes. So I started shooting films, martial arts things, and choreographing fights. Then I realised the fights looked great, but on the screen they looked awful. I began to realise what was involved in directing and became fascinated. So I moved completely away from the type of thing that I was originally interested in doing and became immersed in film.

Could you tell me about going to LA?

When I was shooting my amateur films on video we'd joke whenever we were cutting any crazy corners, 'Corman would love this, Corman would love that.' I saw his studios as being the perfect place to serve an apprenticeship. I went over and worked as an intern there for six months. Corman's company is very small. Yet last year they produced twenty-five features. This year they're going to be producing almost forty. As the company is small, you end up working directly for the different heads of department in the production office, where I worked for three months. You experience production, distribution, international sales, marketing, scripts. It's all accessible within that time.

When did you come back?

I came back in May 1993 to shoot my film *Ties*. The main thing I'd learnt at the Corman studios was that even people at that level just make it up as they go along. There are so few rules. They can get a film into production in under a week from coming up with the idea. Now I can't think of anywhere else that does that. I saw one film where they got the idea to make the film at the end of the week. Over the weekend the script was written – it was a rewrite of an old script that they had. Monday, Tuesday and Wednesday they were casting it and then on Thursday they started shooting. When you experience that kind of thing first hand it makes you realise that it's pointless to mess around for years.

I came back determined to make the film. I sent the usual three letters, actually just two – I didn't even bother with the third – to certain financing places, the Scottish Film Production Fund and British Screen, just for the hell of it. Fortunately I had enough money of my own to shoot it. I'd realised it wasn't going to be as expensive as I had thought. Practically all my equipment was for free and all my facilities too because I did a deal with Grampian Television whereby they had an option to screen the film first, which they're doing in a few months' time. Basically, lab costs, film costs and food were the expenses that were incurred. Plus a few extra pieces of equipment.

One of the people whom I worked with at the Corman studio was the stage manager. We became very good friends. He was interested in coming over to Scotland to help me with the film I wanted to make. He knew a director of photography who read the script and really liked it – the visual elements and so on. He sent over tapes of his work after I had got back to Scotland. I thought he was very good. We spoke over the phone a few times. The first time we ever met was when he arrived in Aberdeen.

How long was the shoot? Where did you do it? Did you have to travel?

It went on for about twenty-one days, six-day weeks. It was all shot in Aberdeen, so it was all very easy to get to. I actually built a set in my garage, which was pretty large. We built the inside of a flat there – we used that quite a lot. Even that cost very little to do because the set panels were already made, recycled from Mel Gibson's *Hamlet* which was shot in the area about two years before. If I'd had more time to prepare we could have got a lot more for free.

Another thing I think is a myth in low-budget independent film-making is not paying the bills until they send the lawyer's letters, pushing it out

73

as far as you can so you'll get that little bit more interest on the money in the bank. Say you push the bills back six months, you're going to gain 2 per cent on the money, or something like that, with current bank rates. If you pay in advance, you just send them a cheque before the work starts, and you can normally knock off 6, 8 or 10 per cent.

Because they know the money's there?

Exactly. They're going on the same principle you are; they know they can put the money in the bank, they can earn the interest on it. Apart from anything else they're not taking the risk of a bad debt. Let's face it, a lot of low-budget film-makers could be seen as a high risk. So that's what I did: I hammered down the rate further and further until we came to a figure and then I named a figure, below their final figure, and I said I'll pay you that now, in advance. I'll send you a cheque a week before the work starts. That kind of preparation beforehand was good, but production was a nightmare. The funny thing is that people who worked on the film, and have worked on other films since, have said it was bliss in comparison to some of the other ones they've worked on.

Tell me about some of the problems.

I was going for the whole method film-making thing. I had a character in the film who was just out of prison – a convicted rapist, unemployed, alcoholic, all that. I had a friend who was the same age as the character, an alcoholic, unemployed, a bit down and out. He had a council flat and I thought that it would make a perfect location. He'd agreed to let us film there. But when I arrived on the day of filming at the location, banging on the door, there was no answer. I kept on banging on the door, everyone was around me and there had been enough shit on the production as it was. I think some people were disenchanted with the project. There I was, banging on the door for ages. I thought the guy was probably sound asleep in his bed after a night's drinking. So I got a ladder and started banging on his first- or second-storey bedroom window. Still there was no answer. Finally I could see that he wasn't in. I couldn't manage to contact him in any other way, so we had to find another location. This was for the biggest scene in the film.

It wasn't until six in the evening that we found another location for three days' filming. This was the flat of somebody else associated with the film. Fortunately the two actors had been rehearsing all through the afternoon. I should have been with them as a director, but I couldn't, because as the producer I was having to find the location. We went in and did the scene which was abnormally long. A twelve-minute scene on the screen, a long dialogue for the end of the film. Very, very dramatic. We filmed the master shot, there were about five of us in the room. As the scene was unfolding, we were exchanging glances, the expression on everyone's face was incredulous, because what was happening in front of us was so powerful. As I stood watching it, for the first time I realised why I was doing the film. Normally you expect to get 80 per cent of what you're hoping for in terms of performance. But from the older actor in the scene I felt I was seeing 110 per cent. It was extraordinary. Absolutely extraordinary and it just compensated for it all.

But there were so many other things, like the big night shoot when we spent two and a half hours with the director of photography perfecting the lighting, three generators working, lighting the whole sequence. Just when we're half-way through the first take, after all this time, the first generator packs up. And then the next generator packs up. Then all three generators start having problems, and it takes us about four hours to sort it out. So we end up shooting from about four in the afternoon through to about eight the next morning. Everyone was absolutely fucked. I was having to cut shots because we were getting more and more behind, owing to the generator problems and the director of photography being so precise about how he was doing things and taking a long time to set things up.

I look at the screen now and I know that it looks very good. But there were a few occasions when it took that little bit too long, so I was having to sacrifice coverage. It's a catch-22 situation: you want it to look as good as it can, but you also want coverage. Apart from anything else, from a diplomatic point of view, he had flown over from LA at his own expense to do the film. He was doing it because he wanted it on his preview reel. He wanted it to look as good as he could make it so I couldn't really bust his balls about it, to shoot faster and faster. Apart from anything else I also wanted it to look as good as possible. But I knew that everyone else in the crew was getting edgy because the days were getting longer and longer and longer.

There was a lot of strain and a lot of pressure. At the end of the third week we lost our sound man because he had to go off to another job. My assistant director ended up taking over the sound. The last few days filming the focus-puller had to go and do another shoot as well. The actors were playing up a bit too. But that's actors for you, that's generally part of their nature, particularly because they're more theatre than film oriented. The young actors who haven't done things on film don't realise how they should pace themselves because they need a lot of stamina. I've recovered. But I haven't been the same person since.

There was one metaphor that came to me when we were doing a night shoot on this old railway line. The rails were no longer there, it was now a long pathway. If you can just imagine this pathway that disappears into darkness and you know it extends for miles and miles. I'm waiting for the lighting to go up and I'm just pacing up and down, up and down this pathway. Every time I walk away from the lights I see this endless path ahead of me. Every time I saw it, I just had this huge urge to keep walking, not to stop, just to walk away from it all and sleep in a field or something like that. Just to abandon it all. The thing was, I knew that to do something like that would be like walking out on my life. It was my script, my production, my money, my direction. I didn't even have an editor on it, I cut the film myself. So with that level of control it was a true auteur film.

Tell me about the post-production.

My whole post-production cost about £500. I had an editing room for free at Grampian Television. There was no time clock on that, so I was in there cutting at my own speed. Sometimes I went in for two hours a day, because I don't like pushing editing and I get bored after a short time. Sometimes they were longer days, six hours or whatever, but never long, long days.

It's a very dialogue-heavy film, a very serious character drama, so it's usually the case that you need a lot of coverage, especially if you're doing close-ups on people. If you're covering reaction as well you're automatically doing 2:1 even if you only do one take on each of them. Robert Rodriguez was in Edinburgh at the festival with *El Mariachi* and I went to that. Afterwards I was mentioning to him that I was just about to start shooting a film. He asked what ratio I was shooting on and I said 8:1. He felt that was too high. But *Ties* is drama and you've got to go with the performances. Action is completely different.

Tell me about the festivals you went to.

It premiered at Edinburgh, played at Hof in Germany with *Shallow Grave* and at Cherbourg where it got best film. It also played at Raindance, with no real attention, no coverage, because there's no meeting system there and there aren't really any buyers showing up.

You're meeting some sales agents and distributors in America. Presumably you're better prepared to deal with them having been a stockbroker?

Definitely. I can talk from the pure business point of view. I know the basics of how to put an equity deal together, for example. I know the way different financial structures work. I think a lot of young film-makers who've gone straight from school to college are intimidated by people in suits because they've never experienced them first hand. They don't know about business. I'm the opposite, that's where I cut my teeth, working on the markets. The high-pressure job in the 80s was trading on the stock market. I worked through a couple of crashes, yet the pressure that you go through on a hard day on the stock market is something like 10 per cent of the average pressure you go through on a film. And you live the film twenty-four hours a day; working on the markets is nine-to-five. Anyone who thinks film-making is an easy endeavour, forget it.

Gary Sinyor

'People just need to be getting out there and making films. That's the only way to revitalise the industry.'

Gary Sinyor is a graduate of the National Film and Television School where he made *Mikey Comes of Age* and *The Unkindest Cut*. The latter was nominated for a BAFTA award in the best short film category. This led to him being commissioned by Eric Idle and Prominent Features to co-write *Leon the Pig Farmer*, a comedy, which he co-produced and co-directed with Vadim Jean. The film received the Evening Standard Award for Best Newcomer, as well as the International Critics Prize at the Venice Film Festival and the Charles Chaplin Prize at the Edinburgh Film Festival. It seemed to be the first high-profile low-budget film produced in the depths of the recent recession, using the Business Expansion Scheme tax-break incentive to raise finance. It has been cited as a source of inspiration by other British producers struggling to raise funds to make their first movie.

Okay, what happened! I went to university; I didn't think I'd stand any chance of being a film-maker but I applied to the BBC and got rejected as everyone does. Then I got a job working for an advertising agency in Manchester that turned out not to be an advertising agency, but a production company. They let me make a couple of freebie films.

What kind of films were they?

I did commercials, really bad commercials. I did a programme for a charity that runs homes for the mentally disabled. I was doing anything I could to stay in work. I had applied to the National Film School as a producer and I got in. Things really took off there. Up to film school film-making was like a dream, but once I got into film school suddenly the dream started to come a little bit closer.

Sam Taylor, a producer who started in sales, said it's really about finding out what people need and giving it to them.

I believed that from very early on. When I went to the National you all have to show the work that got you in. Everyone was showing these incredibly artistic dramas that I didn't understand. I showed them an estate agency commercial and *Dignity*, which was the programme for the mentally disabled. Right from the very early stages I was interested in doing stuff that worked for a specific audience.

Did you get to make your own film?

Yeah! It was a Jewish comedy and it was bought by the BBC. The day that it went out on BBC 2, 4 January 1990, it was seen by Eric Idle, which was a complete fluke. The next day he rang me up and asked me if I had any ideas for feature films.

So how did Leon the Pig Farmer *come together from the Eric Idle stage on?*

It was meant to be a studio film, which somehow or other seems rather unlikely for a film with the title *Leon the Pig Farmer*. I co-wrote it and it went through a number of drafts. Then Eric took it to the States. They rejected it immediately. Then I tried to submit it to all the British companies and the other American companies. I had hysterical meetings where people would tell me that if I could get John Cleese in the lead role, then they'd be able to get the money for me. To which I would say: 'If I could get John Cleese in the lead role, I wouldn't be sitting in your office. I'd be in Universal Studios being wined and dined!' There are some sharky, moronic producers out there.

Then the BBC said they wanted to make it as a mini-series. It was just dragging on. I did a version that was half set in England and half set in America; Yorkshire became Iowa and then it became the Florida Quays. I had the pig farm on the Florida Quays probably because I wanted to go there. What I did was to keep changing elements to try and make the film more worthwhile for investors. Then I met Vadim through my agent. Vadim wanted to do a series and asked to read *Leon the Pig Farmer*. We met once, we met a second time. The third time we met we decided to make *Leon the Pig Farmer*. We literally did the budget on the back of a serviette and went from there.

I'd been introduced to Paul Brooks and we approached him to be executive producer. He said he could raise £50,000 through the BES scheme, which was a 40 per cent tax-break scheme. Vadim, Paul and I worked together on the BES prospectus and started to crew up. We set a date and told ourselves that we were gong to start shooting that date whatever happened and we hit the date. Eric Idle got bought out. We bought the rights back.

Did he give you the idea of making a feature?

He commissioned the script. Between leaving film school and Eric Idle ringing me, I was working at the First Film Foundation. I'd been there for about ten months trying to get things off the ground.

What do you think of First Film?

In principle it's a great idea, although it is to some extent tokenism. The television companies gave money, but mainly as a publicity exercise so that they could be seen to be helping the film industry. The amounts of money they were giving were incredibly small. I don't think they were particularly interested in seeing the First Film Foundation come off. It was a fairly shallow exercise on the part of the people supporting it. But I think the intentions of the people who were working there were very strong and pure.

Do you think that Leon the Pig Farmer *revitalised the British film industry?*

In as much as *Leon* seemed to be the first high-profile low-budget film. There have now been fifteen or so of them, half the British film industry output for the last year and a half. But revitalising the British film industry? I don't think so. I don't think that it has been revitalised. It may be going through a process of revitalisation. I don't think it'll ever be revitalised until you can get away with making a film that doesn't work without being accused of being the death of the British film industry. Every time you make something that doesn't quite come off, you get accused of trying to destroy it! People just need to be getting out there and making films. That's the only way to revitalise the industry.

I'm not sure that going through the process of having some guy tell you over and over again that if you can alter your script a little then maybe you'll get some money is a good one for any film-maker. There comes a point where you think: 'I don't care, the script isn't 100 per cent there, I'll cast it, I'll make a good film, I'll cut it, I'll change bits around. Like every other film-maker in the world I will make mistakes and I hope get it 80 or 90 per cent right.' That's one of the problems with the film industry and the sources of finance we have at present. If they're not happy with absolutely everything, then they won't give you the money. Which I think is counterproductive.

Certainly if you look at the work of a really great film-maker like Woody Allen, he never waits until the script's ready; he goes out, shoots it, comes back, shoots it again. He's all over the shop. I think there's probably just slightly too much emphasis on getting it right in the first place. Which independent film-makers don't need to do. They get it as right as they can and they believe in it. They don't necessarily have to listen to every single person's word of advice.

What was the experience of making Leon the Pig Farmer *like?*

It was brilliant because of Vadim and because of the way that Vadim and
I work together. The shoot was probably the most enjoyable six weeks of
my life. We had a lot of fun. I'd pretty much cast the leads by virtue of
working with Eric Idle. So Brian Glover, Mark Frankel, Janet Suzman
and Gina Bellman were cast before Vadim came on board. Maryam
D'Abo we cast together.

The co-directing process worked very well if the truth be told. Were it
not for the unwillingness of the film industry to accept it, it would
certainly make life as a director a lot easier. Because there are egos
involved, because there is future work involved, because of so many
factors, Vadim and I found it difficult to carry on that way. But if you
asked which way was more enjoyable, I think it would probably be more
enjoyable to do it with someone by you than to do it by yourself.

*Did the process of making the film change you? Some people have said
that the shoot was such an intense experience they weren't the same
afterwards.*

It's changed my life in as much as I spend a lot of time now attending
Jewish charity functions and speaking about how I made *Leon the Pig
Farmer*! I don't think I've changed because of the process. I had the
confidence, I knew that the film was always a good film, I knew that the
script was a good script. I was frustrated afterwards because it took us
four months to get it distributed in the UK and once it was distributed in
the UK I was annoyed because we got some bad reviews and because the
film only took £750,000 when I thought it should have taken £5 million.
Yes, you can say 'I've done it, I've succeeded in making a feature film.'
That is a huge thing, but I don't think it changes you that much. You get
kicks out of it because you see the film on in the cinema, you see it being
reviewed or you see people queuing to go and see it. And because you've
made one film, it becomes easier to make another.

How many cinemas did Leon the Pig Farmer *play in?*

Opened in six and went up to twenty-eight.

And Solitaire for 2?

Opened in forty-six and I think it's down to twelve. It's gone the other
way. It's done terribly. As far as I'm concerned the critics have killed the
film. It's interesting how well it's doing in foreign sales. It's causing a stir
because the critics have really savaged the film; I keep meeting people
who really liked the film. But it's probably not edgy enough for the
critics. I'm not Quentin Tarantino, I never wanted to be. The critics can
kill films. They've killed *Solitaire for 2*. We can have arguments about

what we could or should have done, but I think the audience awareness of the film was quite high. I think the film doesn't deserve to be seen by only a few people. There are a lot of people who would enjoy the film if they went to see it.

The audience are so geared towards American films, they don't seem inclined towards British ones.

I think the problem isn't so much the British films. I think the problem is that *Solitaire for 2* is a romantic comedy, which is an old-fashioned style of film. There are a lot of people out there who would like to go and see a film like that. But generally, they're not critics. There are people out there who will go and sit there and say, 'This is a great film. Why don't they make films like this any more?' It's why Whitney Houston gets to number one with 'I Will Always Love You'. She's not some edgy group like the Dead Coffins, or whatever they call themselves, that you happen to listen to when you're down at the Acid House or whatever. What gets to number one for ten weeks is Whitney Houston singing 'I Will Always Love You' or Wet Wet Wet singing 'Love Is All Around'. This is mainstream stuff. It's popular.

We're losing the audience, that's the problem. Why should the public bother to go when every film is of a particular type? So they switch off, they don't bother to think about going to the cinema any more. The only film that broke through was *Four Weddings and a Funeral*. It wasn't because people went to see *Four Weddings and a Funeral* ten times that it did ten times as well. It did ten times as well because the people who normally don't go to the cinema went to the cinema. They all said, 'Great! I can finally go and see a film with my fifty-year-old husband or my fifty-year-old wife or with my ten-year-old kid.' They all jumped up and down and said, 'Great! A film that's got good publicity and nice people in it. It must be funny.' And they all trotted along to the cinema.

What are you doing next?

Monty Python meets Merchant Ivory. I can't stand the British class films going on endlessly, one after the other, so we're taking the piss out of them. And after that there's a thriller and after that a comedy and then ... I doubt I'll ever be doing *Judge Dredd 3*.

Ray Brady

'You can make a film in this country with no money whatsoever.'

Ray Brady and Jim Crosbie wrote the film *Boy Meets Girl* with the aim of criticising the inept way violence is classified in this country. It was intended to start a debate about the British Board of Film Classification's policy of not allowing realistic violence to be portrayed on screen, while rarely cutting 'action violence'. This policy has since been challenged. There have been changes on the Board, which now intends to look much more closely at action movie violence and to be more careful about films that may be glamorising violence. *Boy Meets Girl* was not given a certificate, although Ray Brady is prepared to contest this decision in any way necessary. The film has recently found a Japanese distributor and Ray Brady has since directed *Little England,* a documentary about the attitudes of young people to current controversial topics.

I finished school at eighteen and applied to Poly in Liverpool. I did a year and realised that I didn't want to become a building surveyor, it was boring. I went to a lot of gigs during the day. Liverpool was really kicking at the time, it was about 1983 or 1984. I dropped out, bummed around, travelled, got jobs in France picking grapes and stuff like that for a few months.

Then I came back to my home town and picked up my father's business, which was plastering. I got fed up with that and went to Italy, where I was doing Italian wall veneers, putting colour and patterns in plaster and waxing it. I came back, and there weren't many people who could do that. So I ended up starting an international plastering company, doing contracts as far away as Hawaii.

I was getting older, working incredibly hard. I'd come home, sit down, plonk myself in front of the video. Well first of all TV, then I got a bit more discriminating and started getting into video. Soon I was developing certain tastes, becoming a film buff I suppose. Before long I started getting the itch to do my own stuff.

What was the strategy behind your first film?

When you're making a first film with very little money, you should do something that people want. Something that you would want to watch. Make it a genre movie. Try to set it all in one location. It's a classic movie cliché, but it works: find a big house somewhere and make a story around that one house. You don't have to worry about permits and licences and loss of equipment and all that. If you've got a camera which you've borrowed from someone personally you may not have to insure it at all. Insurance is one of the large costs on a low-budget production. If you've got it all contained within one big house or one area, then your insurance costs come down.

The hardest part is getting the film in the can; after that it's downhill all the way. There are many different hats you have to wear along the way. You have to figure out how to promote your film, how to get a sales agent. You have to go to film markets and understand how they work, and festivals too.

One of our main problems has been the British Board of Film Classification [BBFC], whom we first ran into when we were about to get a distribution deal from Metro Tartan. Provisionally we had a deal from Metro Tartan for film and video rights for *Boy Meets Girl*. We were happy with it. We went to the Berlin Film Festival, expecting to sign the deal on return. We went there looking for foreign sales, but people were waiting for our certification in England. Because if you can't get classification in your country of origin it looks as if you've got a dodgy film. People have been holding off for that reason, as far as I can discern. So we got back from Berlin, and Metro Tartan had presented the film to the BBFC. That's where our troubles began, because the BBFC's view was that the film could never be released on video.

The BBFC said that a) they didn't understand the film or why we'd want to make it and b) that the film would never, ever get a video release. They told this to Metro Tartan and Metro suspended our deal. So for the last nine months we've been trying to hold people off while we sort this out.

Before Christmas we rang up the BBFC. They claimed never to have said the film would not get a video release! I was shocked. I could have said, 'Excuse me but you've just messed up my whole life for nine months and put my career on hold because of what you said to Metro Tartan. Now you say that you never said it.' What can you do? I bit the bullet and said, 'So there is a possibility of getting a video release?' The BBFC said I should present the film again. The reason why they changed their minds, as far as I can tell, is because we went through loads of film festivals to increase public awareness of what we were doing. The BBFC realised that other people were taking the film seriously.

Britain is the most censored country in the whole of the Western hemisphere. They call it 'classification'. But 'classification' is only an accurate description of the films that the BBFC passes. The word 'censored' should be used for films that are completely banned, such as ours. As far as I'm concerned, the BBFC means the British Board of Film Censorship.

The fact is that journalists here think it's quite an important film. Derek Malcolm who originally didn't like the film has come around to it. He even called it the English answer to *Man Bites Dog*. Alexander Walker and Tony Rayns support it. These are some of the major critics in this country. Part of the reason we made the film was to criticise the BBFC. The film has been a sore spot for them over the last nine months.

We could have rolled over and died, gone away or stopped the film and started making another one or something. But because we kept on hitting the press they have been forced to give us another hearing. It's embarrassing for them. *Sight and Sound* did an article about censorship with a direct reference to us, saying how unfair it was that *Natural Born Killers* got a full Board viewing, whereas we didn't. They pointed out that it's an insignificant amount of money to the producers of *Natural Born Killers* to re-edit and change that film. But for us it would be financially prohibitive.

What about finding people to work on the film when there's not a lot of money around?

There were people who came on board and then dropped out. There were people who came and worked brilliantly for the three weeks of production. Then that was it. They were gone and they haven't helped us since. It's idealism you're looking for. You look for dedication, the amount of hours people put in. Very simply, if someone is working towards becoming a cinematographer, if they're putting in five hours a week, or ten hours a week or twelve or fifteen, you know they're not going to be a cinematographer unless they're really lucky or really rich or just a genius. But if they're doing eighty or ninety hours a week and doing loads of reading and research, then they are more likely to get to be what they want to be.

If you're not in production then you should be working on other people's film, or in post-production. I want to make a commercially viable film now, with no controversy. I've proved I can deliver a feature. But I've still got to clear up some debts. Then I can start accounts and have credit access to a large amount of money, probably two or three times more than I had before.

You can turn around a film really quickly. If you can get it through post-production and get it out and about through the festival circuit, you can deal with it in six months. It's when you delay that creditors are a problem. I'm not afraid of taking out large amounts of money on credit. But it's much easier if you do something which is less controversial. Then you know that you will get that money back quickly. Over six months, most people can cut you the slack in the film industry. But when it gets up to nine months to a year, then people start getting edgy. You can make a film in this country with no money whatsoever. I could be easily through a second film by now, planning a third one, if it hadn't been for the censorship problems with *Boy Meets Girl*. But it was something we felt we had to say. So we did it anyway.

Our financial pressure isn't, of course, the BBFC's concern. But if the BBFC were a real business they would never get away with the way they deal with film-makers. They take whatever time they want, they stall, they just leave things hanging. The BBFC say they are reliant upon fees and money. I tried to have the fee waived because I'm a full-time degree student. But they said they couldn't do that for anyone. I suspect that the major studios are such big clients for the BBFC that they can't mess them around too much. Independent film-makers just get pushed to the back of the queue.

Andrew Macdonald

'Our films are made for the British market. That's the only way you'll ever have any kind of British film industry.'

Andrew Macdonald was born in Glasgow in 1966 and went to a boarding school in Perthshire. He made his first film on Super 8 at school, at the time *Chariots of Fire* was being filmed in the hills nearby. Excited by what was happening in film, he opted not to go to university and instead moved to London and began helping out at the National Film and Television School. A chance meeting with the screenwriter John Hodge led to the collaboration that has so far produced the hit films *Shallow Grave* and *Trainspotting*.

I got into film when I left school. I came down to London and tried to get a job in Soho as a runner, and then I went to the National Film School because somebody told me that you can get work there, experience on films. So that's what I did, I worked on a film there for free. I was lucky because my dad was working in London at the time and I had a place to stay. I was under the impression that I could get a place at the National at eighteen, or whatever, just coming out of school not having done anything, but it was a good place to start. I started working on other people's films and for other production companies, working my way up towards location manager, and eventually decided to produce.

How did you meet John Hodge and Danny Boyle?

I met John Hodge by chance when I was directing a short film. His sister was one of the editors. She said my brother is a doctor but wants to be a scriptwriter, you're struggling as a film-maker/producer, you two should get together. So we met and he had the idea for *Shallow Grave* and started writing it and we worked on it for about fifteen months. Then we took it to Channel Four and they asked about who was going to direct it. We had the idea already or I had the very strong idea that we didn't want Stephen Frears, we wouldn't have wanted someone as successful as

Danny Boyle has become now. So we went out and met all the young directors who had directed something, and it was really about finding somebody whom we got on with, who could bring their own interpretation but at the same time understood what we were trying to do. As I've said a few times I wasn't really a fan of *Mr Wroe's Virgins*, which Danny directed. I did admire it, but that wasn't what was important. We got on with Danny. He understood what we were trying to do with the film.

Why do you particularly want to make films in Britain? Why make films anyway?

God knows. Sometimes I ask myself that. I think I'm quite good at working with people. I get on with most people. I can get people to do things. That must have something to do with it. Making films in Britain? Just because that's where we started, it's where we come from. I don't feel very nationalistic but I don't see the point of going to America. I went for a while, for nine months, worked for a production company in LA and enjoyed it very much. That was before *Shallow Grave*, in 1986. If I was going to stay that would have been the time to stay. I think it's very difficult. Now we've only just started going back there: we're going to make our next film in America. I just don't want to be like everybody else there. It's much easier being a wannabe here. Now, I hope, with our bit of success we'll be able to go back there and make films on our terms. I think it's a real danger to go there and end up doing something you don't really want to do, or be in a situation where you don't know what you're doing. That's why we decided to make *Trainspotting* after *Shallow Grave*.

Did you particularly admire Irvine Welsh's novel [Trainspotting]*?*

Yeah. I particularly admired the novel. I thought it was great material for a film. I was very keen for us to do something small, something that didn't involve a large amount of money, something that didn't involve having to kowtow to studios and stars and money men and stuff like that. That was more important, so that we were able to express ourselves. So people understood that it was the film that was important. It wasn't the director or whatever else. It was the team and it was the film. We could have made a genre piece or something like that. It's a suspense thriller. It's an unusual one, it breaks lots of rules. We've made two potential crossover films. There are three types of films really. There's the art film – Greenaway, or *Il postino* and stuff like that – which tends to be for an older audience. It's quality production. Then there's crossover like ours, or like *The Usual Suspects* – more intelligent than the mainstream but not as difficult as the art. Then there's the mainstream, one of the most difficult. Real mainstream is *Die Hard* and *Aliens*, stuff like that which is great. The problem is there's so much other stuff which is just terrible. I think you can only make mainstream if you have Harrison Ford and Julia Roberts – you've got to go the whole way. *Shallow Grave* was playing with mainstream movie genres but giving them a twist and that's what we're into doing. We admire the American independents.

We don't have that kind of film-making here; we've never had it. We try to do mainstream and they're always terrible. People kowtow to Hollywood values, but we can't go the whole way. The only films we've made that are good are art films but they're very limited.

Are there any decisions that you made as a producer on Shallow Grave *that you're especially proud of?*

Hiring Danny Boyle. That was a pretty smart move. Making it in Scotland, making it for a million pounds. Fitting the aesthetics around the budget by working with the writer and director who understood it. The production designer was my decision whereas the cameraman and editor were people Danny had worked with before. My key references were *Blood Simple* and *Metropolitan* and *Blue Velvet*. Stuff like that. I was targeting the audience for the sort of films that I like and want to see, not just the ones I admire.

What kind of role do you play when a film is being shot?

Once filming begins it's really the world of the director and all the producer can do to change things is to sack people, and on a low-budget film you can't do that. It never really gets to that stage where you end up just being, controlling ... you just get to say no a lot, saying you know what time it is and you know what we have to do today. It's a very unsatisfying job really. I worked on the script with John before we worked with Danny and at the end I work with the editor a lot. The decisions I make, the budget, where we're going to shoot it. The general tone and setting up and carrying that through, how much people are being paid, who we hire, the type of person, the risks we go to. A lot of the time John and I are working on other ideas. I hate the shooting to be honest but it's only six weeks out of a two-and-a-half-year process.

Are you happy producing?

Very happy ... all I'm trying to do is build up a team. Not just of writer and director, but cameraman, editor, designer, actors. And not just the same ones. Danny and I are going to executive produce a film this year. We try to do things that are risky, that are British, that can't be done by anybody else. Even if that means that our next film with John and Danny is set in America – it's our view of America, an outsider's view. That kind of thing is what makes it interesting, worth doing. We don't, like most other film companies, develop a lot of stuff. We've got three things in development and they'll all be made. We just concentrate on that and have a very sure sense of whether it's right or wrong. We've got *A Life Less Ordinary*, which is John's, a film called *Pretty Shitty City*, which is shooting in June, written by Kevin Allen, who's also going to direct it, and another called *Jam*, written by Biyi Bandele Thomas and set in Brixton. We're completely independent, we have no overhead ties, nothing. We're always in discussion with people, looking for a good deal, but I look around and don't see one overhead deal that's working, particularly in this town. We'll probably eventually get some kind of private investment from a bank or something like that. If we move into making mainstream movies, then I think we should get a studio deal. Anything in between doesn't seem to be very successful. The worst thing that you can do is show people your ideas too early, which is why I don't think 'first look' deals are any good.

It's a case of mulling things over, rewriting, changing things. A process which is absolutely fundamental for a low-budget film. That's why we're not rushing into doing anything else at the moment.

Were you surprised by the success of Shallow Grave?

I wasn't surprised. I knew it would be a financial success but I never knew it would do £5 million at the box-office. I don't think people really appreciate how good that is. *The Madness of King George* is not a British film, *Sense and Sensibility* is not a British film; they're all funded by Americans, made for the American market. Our films are made for the British market. That's the only way you'll ever have any kind of British film industry. Its the one thing I don't think we get enough recognition for. And it's perfectly possible. You just have to try and make films for the British market. *Carry On* films are better than all these period plays. It's not about tax breaks or the Lottery. Look at the films that are being made with Lottery money. It's ridiculous; they're just more of the same. They have to pay for themselves. There are too many films in the world, though of course I'd complain bitterly if mine weren't being made!

Paul Brooks

'You've got to Smash down the door and slap the script on people's desks.'

Paul Brooks went to Pinner Grammar School and London University, where he studied English and philosophy. He has always loved films and architecture and moved in film producing with three other film lovers he met when working in the property business. After executive producing *Leon the Pig Farmer*, he formed the production company Metrodome with £12,000. He went on to produce *Beyond Bedlam*, *Clockwork Mice* and *Proteus* and co-executive produce *Solitaire for 2*. He has just executive produced *Killing Time* which has been picked up by Columbia TriStar. Metrodome has been floated on the London Stock Exchange and is now capitalised at around £6 million. For him, film, like any other business venture, is a matter of being positive.

How did you become a producer?

Do you mean philosophically or practically?

Practically.

Just got on the phone and raised the money. Found a script that I liked enough to raise the money for.

What problems did you encounter when you started to make films?

Just the problems you encounter in any business. Trying to raise the money to make a product you believe in is always hard whatever you're making, be it movies or widgets. To be honest, film's no different to any other business. You make things happen or you don't make things happen. It's just a function of personality. There's no great trick to it, you want to do it, then you do it.

A friend of mine recently said film-making's easy. It's getting the money that's hard. I agree with that to an extent.

Sorry no, that's an incredibly stupid thing to say. Because making films is incredibly fucking hard. Most films don't work. Eight films out of ten don't work. It's an incredibly hard art form.

Would you agree that Leon the Pig Farmer *helped revitalise the British film industry to some extent?*

Maybe. It was made in the depths of the recession. The only way we could make it was to do it for very little money, get everybody to defer their payment and just beg, steal and borrow. It grabbed people's attention and imagination because it proved that you can do it. It kick-started things. People thought, 'Well, if they can do it, we can do it.'

I think things are starting to happen more now.

It's a good time, the best time for years, best time for donkey's years here, no question. It's a brilliant time. But the number of people who jump on it will be very small, because culturally we're a hopeless nation when it comes to being entrepreneurial in film. We're just a very negative culture. People should be trying to bring about change in the grass-roots film-making culture.

You know the reason that the Americans do so well at what they do is that they're very positive. The only thing that makes things happen is positivity. Everything else is completely irrelevant. You can take a modicum of talent as given. People get ground down here by everybody saying, 'you can't, you can't, you can't, you can't'. That's our biggest problem. That's why very few people will break through, even in this very exciting time, because we're too timid. It's: 'Could you possibly look at this script for me?' – 'No!' You've got to smash down the door and slap the script on people's desks. Get on the phone, drive them mad. It's the only way. Life is short, so just get on with it. What's the worst thing that can happen? You make a crappy film. So what? Go and do another one, a bit better.

Unless you're doing it, you're never going to make a *good* film. The bottom line is people just don't have the bollocks for it. You've got to strip naked and jump in the deep end. Everybody skirts around the outside and fafs around and drinks coffee and says 'let's redo this' and 'the script isn't right yet'. Of course, that may be the case. But often it's the excuse. There are plenty of people who make one film and never make another because they lose perspective and because it's a very tough business. The only way to deal with it is to be tough.

When you say 'lose perspective' what do you mean?

Perhaps they think it's all going to be easy once the first film is made. It isn't.

91

What's your agenda every morning?

Well, we do what a film production company does. We look at scripts, we do deals, we talk deals. Time is always a problem. You just have to deal with it as efficiently as you can. I'm always behind, but that's just a function of the job. I'm sure every other business is the same. You never have enough time, you're always running against the clock. It's high stress. But you're either into that or you're not.

How long did it take to prepare Leon the Pig Farmer?

Most pre-production is about six to eight weeks.

How many people did you have on it?

Sixty or seventy.

Where did you shoot the film?

In and around London. A week in Yorkshire.

How did Leon the Pig Farmer *do commercially?*

It did pretty well here, not so well everywhere else. It did very well in Australia. It did enough of a job to do what we needed it to do.

Where did you get the money? Did you sell it to them on the basis that they'd get money back?

From private investors. You sell to them on whatever basis you can, which is that you think it's a good deal. You think that you've cut the risks as low as you can, you think that they will get their money back. But that there are no guarantees.

It's really simple. The mechanics of it are a piece of cake. You have to be ballsy and aggressive. Nicely aggressive. There's no great secret to it. It's just cutting through all the shit and getting to the bottom line which is 'Here's a script that I believe in. So how am I going to raise the money?' Then just figure out a thousand ways to raise the money. If they don't work, figure out another thousand, two thousand, three thousand. Get a phone book and call every single person in the phone book.

The only way that these things happen is through energy. Energy and positivity. Energy will make a bad script happen and no energy will leave a good script lying on the shelf. It's the whole thing of getting people enthused, getting people to have confidence in you, and then delivering. In a business that's full of shit, it's about delivering. The reason why, touch wood, people now come to me with interesting propositions is because in three and a half years I've delivered six films and floated

Metrodome on the London Stock Exchange. When I started I said I'd deliver three in three years. Everybody said that was impossible. That's more a statement about people's nervousness here, and this cultural fear and timidity, than a statement about how great I am.

You have to set a date. I mean my simple answer to somebody who says, 'How do I make my first film?' is that you set a date and make it. If you have to start and you've got three quid in the bank, start; if you can only do one day's shooting it doesn't matter, start this weekend. Borrow a 16mm camera from somebody. Start. What we do here is make excuses all the time. It's all bullshit. The only way is to just do it. It's incredibly hard, but it's incredibly simple. It fundamentally revolves around energy. It revolves around force of personality, it revolves around nice bullying, cajoling, schmoozing and all that. I also hope at the end of the day it revolves around being honourable and straight with people.

But perhaps one of the reasons I've been fortunate so far is that I'm a maverick. I'm from outside the industry, I'm not typical. I don't have time for the shit. So I'm disarmingly frank with people, which saves me a lot of time. If people think I'm an asshole, well, I can live with that. The thing is that it's hard, it's major, major, major stress. You've got to be tough, you've got to be able to hang in there when the shit's flying. You can educate yourself to be like that, but over here we're just too timid. It's ... rraaaaarrggh! Get it on!

Mike Sarne

'Big films are being cancelled all over the place. People think they've got it all together and it falls apart ... I think a young person who has no track record at all is in an easier position than someone who's got a terrific track record.'

Mike Sarne is the writer, producer and director of *The Punk and the Princess*. He began his career as a pop singer in the 60s. When his manager went bust he decided he had to find a new profession so he became a photographer, which led to work as a cameraman on commercials. He has directed five films, *Road to Saint Tropez*, *Joanna*, *Myra Breckinridge*, *Intimacy* and *The Punk and the Princess*, which is his latest film, made with a group of young film-makers. In the 60s, one of the main difficulties for aspiring film-makers was union regulations; today it is finding financial backing.

For my first film, back in the 60s, I managed to borrow ten grand. I won't go into all the dickering around. It's a long story. I don't know if you've got enough tape in the recorder.

Getting the money is one of the themes of this book.

It's a very interesting story. I had the film idea, right? I knew a guy who had invented a thing called 'bond washing'. It was a loophole. The government issued bonds, saying you wouldn't lose money if you sold these bonds. What he had picked up on was that he could sell them to his own company, get the dividends and still own the bonds! Like the hooker who gives it away and keeps it. In about four or five months he'd made a quarter of a million pounds. Then the government started getting suspicious.

He invented something else he called Constellation. In those days people paid vast tax. You had to pay 80 or 90 per cent of your surplus earnings as tax. People were leaving the country in droves because they couldn't stand the tax system. His idea was that you put your earnings above a certain living allowance into a public company, which was quoted on the stock exchange. You were allocated shares in that public company. You couldn't be taxed for those earnings because the company that was representing you would receive all the money. The shares could only be taxed under capital gains tax, which was about 30 per cent. A great scheme. He got a whole host of celebrities, all the people in England who had any money, to go for it. I was one of his potential marks. He'd call me up every so often.

He invited me out to his home, a weekend, or maybe it was just lunch on Sunday with his wife and family. I went out there and talked about the idea I had to make a film. He called me during the next week and said he'd like to talk further. I told him that I was casting, I had the lead but I still needed a young man. The female lead was the wife of Basil Dearden; he was a great director, who did *The Blue Lamp* and a few other things. He was a friend of mine and he encouraged me. I acted for him in a film called *A Place to Go*, which I starred in with Rita Tushingham. It was Andy Warhol's favourite film but it didn't do any business . . . I was very involved with the making of it. Basil took me under his wing and he encouraged me to take an interest in the technical side of film-making. His wife's name was Melissa Stribling. She did a lot of horror films with Peter Cushing.

A few months go by. The money man gets back to me and says, 'Would you like to come down to my place in the south of France to discuss the film? We'll have more time to sit back and you can explain to me what it's all about. Take the plane to Nice. I'll send you the ticket.' I was dumbfounded, but he insisted. I got off the plane and his car was there. We start shooting off down the road towards Antibes and he says, 'I've got to tell you something, Mike. There are some men who like boys.' At this point I want to get out of the car and hoof it back to the airport. . . . Anyway, he started telling me about his disastrous love affairs. 'I'm in love with a boy and it's driving me crazy. And he loves someone else. No he doesn't . . . it's just someone else is after him, and I want him. What I want you to do, Mike, is to tell me if you think he might be suitable for your film.' I'm really trying to keep him amused, keep him interested. So I saw the boy, who met us down there, and I said I'd test him. The next week he was flown to London and I took some pictures of him with Melissa, which I think were published in *Films and Filming*.

The guy's company were all ready to invest, the completion guarantors were brought in. We had to start assembling a good crew from the best studios. I went around to the union and I said, 'I'm not a member of the ACTT, but please let me make the film. I'm the producer and the writer and the director. I'm getting the money. I'm not asking to be a member of the union. Just let me make it, I'll make sure your members will get paid.' I was terribly frightened. The next day my union ticket came, pushed under my door! So I put the schedule together. Come the day we're supposed to leave, the cheque still hasn't arrived. My friend who'd set the deal up is now in bad odour. The government had plugged the loophole. Everybody was calling him a crook, saying, 'How dare he run this scam?', and they were sacking him from the company. They didn't want to have anything to do with his schemes.

While the crew were waiting to get on a plane to film in France, I went down to the money men's office and said, 'What the fuck is this? I've got a crew waiting to get on a plane, I've got people in the south of France. You haven't come up with the money. What am I supposed to do? I've committed a crew, they can sue me for everything. They can sue me for their wages even if the film doesn't get made. I've ordered the stock, that company can sue me. It's money I don't have because when you're making films you go broke in order to make the bloody things.' I'm getting the stonewall English bullshit treatment. I thought, 'Alright, there's nothing I can do.' I put my papers back in my briefcase, closed it and walked to the door. I said, 'I've only got one more thing to say to you guys. You're not gentlemen.' They chased me down the corridor! Grabbed me by the arms. Pulled me back. And gave me the money. Just because I said they weren't gentlemen!

Money, if it's ten grand or ten million dollars, brings the same nasty human qualities out. People try to stop you doing what you want to do. Everyone has these problems. Big films are being cancelled all over the place. People think they've got it all together and it falls apart. Everybody goes through the most humiliating crap. Often there's no good reason why a film is cancelled. You've just got to have a nose for the money. See where it is, see who's got it and don't believe too much of the bullshit. I think a young person who has no track record at all is in an easier position than someone who's got a terrific track record.

I had lunch with a legendary Hollywood director a few months ago who shall remain nameless and I suggested a couple of ideas which he turned down rather rudely. Later on, I went to an agent and I said that I had had lunch with this man and he really wasn't very friendly. There he is, an old man but he's got all his marbles, he's directed some of the best films ever made. And the agent said to me that he'll never work again. I was surprised. This director's worth millions, tens of millions. I realised that his rudeness to me was indicative of the way he was treating other people. Although he thought of himself as a pillar of Hollywood society, everybody respects him and lifetime achievement awards are coming out his ears, he can't work. I went to another agent the next day, and they said, 'It's true, he'll never work again.'

In the whole system the people are so shallow and materialistic. Everything is a knee-jerk, they love you one minute and hate you the next. You shouldn't take any of them seriously. You shouldn't take their rejection seriously any more than you should take their approval seriously. A young director who has made a ten-minute short is in just as good a position as a Hollywood legend. There's no difference. In fact, you would have a better chance than the above-mentioned Hollywood legend, no question. Because they've decided that he will never work again. Same way they've decided that Mike Sarne won't make another film in Hollywood. They're very nice to me, have lunch with me, see my films, pat me on the back, say 'Great stuff, Mike'. What they don't say is, 'You won't work here again, Mike.'

You don't know what the key is that's going to open up the money. I think clever PR and the right connections are more important than talent as far as getting a deal together is concerned. That being said, the work I've got has been because I've got enough technique to solve problems other people can't. You have to have technique. And you have to have imagination to turn things like *Myra Breckinridge* into a movie. A lot of people tried to write *Myra Breckinridge*; they spent a million or more before I came on the picture. But being well connected is important too, and having the right people like your work is very important.

Tell me about The Punk and the Princess. *How did you get it together?*

I had the script in my bottom drawer for years. I couldn't set it up when I bought the rights originally. I wanted to make a punk film back in the punk era. Everybody around me was very excited about it. I bought the rights. People said it was a commercial idea. These days, if the same phenomenon happened, maybe we could do it. I was going through my own emotional problems. My marriage had been breaking up, my teenage kids were growing up, and I really wanted to understand the problems about drugs and teenage rebellion and alienation. What I liked about *The Punk* was that it looked at grown-ups from a kid's point of view: 'They're full of shit, they're a bunch of phoneys. Maybe they want what's best for us but the way they go about it is short sighted!' That jived perfectly with Romeo and Juliet. They've got well-meaning parents acting like schmucks and fucking up the children's lives.

The Punk became a script that I would send time-wasters to tell them to fuck off. Because it was full of swearwords, it's full of obscenity, it's full of fuck you – it's *The Punk*! For twenty years I would send it out to people, a nicely printed script, and the first thing on it is: 'The Punk Band is on stage and it's "One two fuck you ... I can't do the things that I want to do, I don't know the people I want to know ..."' Very punky attitude. I was quite happy with the script, very angry, very rude, very antisocial, very anti-everybody, very revolutionary, very anarchic, the essence of punk. So someone came along asking if I had any scripts. So I thought, 'There's this thing called *The Punk*. He can have a look at that. He can read the script and I'll never be bothered again.' He came round the next morning:

'This is great, I love it.' First person who's ever loved it, first person who's ever seen any merit in it. I'm a bit suspicious.

'Can you afford it?'

'How much is it going to cost?'

'I don't know. About £400,000?'

He made a downward gesture with his hands. So I said: '£350,000?'

He repeated the gesture.

'£300,000?'

He kept miming 'down' with his hands, pushing downwards, without saying anything. '£250,000?' I think it's a joke now. I've given him the least I think a low-budget film can be made for – £400,000. BBC plays cost about £800,000, and here he is asking me to make a feature film. Laughing, I said, 'What? £200,000?'. He says 'Yeah' and he puts his thumb up like this! 'You're going to give me £200,000 to make this film?' 'Yeah.' 'Okay.'

Because of the budgetary restraint a lot of the stuff couldn't be shot. It was to have been a film that would evoke the 70s. I'd have had to worry about costumes and wardrobe and continuity and all kinds of stuff. I thought to get round this, I would shoot it in a semi-documentary style, keep within the budget. Update the punk to a punk-type kid around these days, keep a sense of immediacy but not lose the core. So he came up with his £200,000, and eventually the budget crept up and it cost about £400,000 like I said in the first place.

Nothing you do is perfect unless you're really fortunate in having everything you want. Films are always a compromise. I'm very happy with *The Punk and the Princess* in that I feel it's a cohesive whole. It's true to itself, the shape is right and it makes sense according to its own logic, which is what I wanted. We made it independently. I didn't own the company but now they've landed me with the company as well. We haven't had an awful lot of money to promote it. But we're just soldiering on with it. We made the money ourselves, paid for it ourselves, borrowed the money ourselves.

I'm trying to get together a group of young film-makers who want to make their first feature films. With the English, everybody will try and stop you doing what you want to do. Everybody. Your wife, your mother, your friends, the ones who are pretending to be friendly and to help you, will do what they can to fuck you up, intentionally or unintentionally. They will not let you make your film. No one wants to let you do what you want to do in life! No one. You've got to learn this thing that Paul Newman spoke about, 'Bounce-backability'. When you get rejected or disappointed, you've got to bounce right back. It's got to be like water off a duck's back. You'll find the waves will part as long as you're determined. Determination is probably the most important quality. There are people who'll give you cameras. You can get film stock, it's not such a mystery, getting hold of film stock. You can get actors. So, you're a long way towards making a movie. You can make a feature film.

Brianna Perkins

'We're not drama programming, we're not children's programming. We're something unique.'

Brianna Perkins was born in Holland and until she was fourteen years old was educated in Italy. Back in England she went to Roedean School, then spent a year at the Sorbonne in Paris studying French civilisation. She has a degree in psychology from Brunel University. An accountancy course led her into the accounts department of a special effects company. She moved on to become a charity administrator for the Children's Film Unit and produced her first film *Under the Bed* in 1988. At the Unit, children from all sorts of different backgrounds come together to attend workshops where they are instructed in the craft skills necessary to produce a feature film before writing and making their own films which are shown on Channel Four. The Children's Film Unit plays an important part in ensuring a continued high level of commitment to the film and TV industry in this country over the generations.

At the moment we have eighty children coming to our workshops every Saturday. We teach them all aspects of 16mm film-making. We also do animation. We used to have a drama workshop but we abandoned that because we wanted to expand the technical side, so we have a junior and a senior technical workshop. We now have a sixteen-plus group, for those who have been in our workshops for a number of years and want to carry on making their own films. We are also starting a video unit for our sixteen-plus group.

We teach them everything: camera, sound, lighting, editing. We have script workshops at the beginning of the year. The youngsters are involved in the writing of the script, which we then present to Channel Four. That process takes about three months. It's actually the kids who write the scripts. We tell them to think of maybe five topics over the Christmas holiday. They come back with all sorts of ideas and the group chooses the best idea, which should also be the most financially feasible. That's the script group – roughly fifteen children – which gets reduced to a much smaller group when it comes to the actual writing. So if they have an idea about fighter planes, they can forget it, because we're not going to get the money to do it. But we also like them to choose a subject that is important to them, because it's a big opportunity for the kids, they can say something that they feel really strongly about to the rest of the world. We get two million viewers. Our films are shown in Europe and all over the world. So this is a big opportunity for them to say something important and be listened to.

Willie's War was an anti-war film. It's about class and it's anti-war, something they feel very strongly about. *The Higher Mortals* is about the educational system. We've also done environmental thrillers. They're all quite hard hitting. Yes, kids do smoke and drink and take drugs, and all of that is involved in our films. This has never been a problem with David Aukin, the Head of Drama at Channel Four.

Our films were seen as family films. Now that we've been moved to a children's slot our films don't fit and they are telling us that we can't have any swearing. 'Bloody' is not allowed; smoking is not allowed; they say, 'You can't have children drinking in your films.' We've had a big debate about this and our kids are up in arms about it. I mean they're not ten years old – well some of them are – but they range from ten to eighteen and it tends to be the fourteen and fifteen-year-olds who are doing the scriptwriting. They are not films for children; they are family films for the age group twelve and over. So we're having a battle with Channel Four about that. We hope that they'll see us as a special case. We're not drama programming, we're not children's programming. We're something unique.

How well known is the Unit?

We started in 1981 and we've made roughly one film a year. So we're one of the most prolific film companies in this country. We are not well known but our profile is slowly increasing. We get a lot of publicity when we actually shoot the films during the summer, because it's kids behind cameras. So slowly our profile is increasing.

Our president is Prince Edward. We've just got Steven Spielberg as a vice-president. Lord Attenborough is involved and David Puttnam too. So, with such big names, word is getting about and the press are suddenly quite interested. I talk to people and they do know about us. Every year we do a big Royal Premiere to raise funds to run the workshops. That attracts a lot of publicity. All our films are shown at all the children's film festivals abroad. *Willie's War* won the prize at the European Youth Film Festival last weekend. And that was worth £2,500 in cash and a distribution deal. I've travelled quite a lot with the films and they all ask me how to start up a Children's Film Unit. The problem is always financing, getting somebody committed enough to start it up.

Are the films well distributed?

Normally we sell to television, sometimes to cinema. The British Council bought six of our films to show all over the world in schools. It's some money. We have to make money to keep it going. We need to raise about £50,000 to run the workshops and the premises every year. We don't get any money from the government. The *Evening Standard* has helped us for the last three years. Sony and Kodak give us a couple of thousand a year, but it's a struggle. Our premieres raise about ten thousand. Sometimes we make two films a year.

What is special about children making films?

Because they are learning they don't mind being criticised. Before they work on a feature they will work in the workshops for about two years and will have learnt a lot. By the time we let them loose on a feature they have to know what they're doing because it's very, very expensive. The pounds are just whirring away.

We will have, for example, in the camera department, two juniors and two seniors. The seniors will be teaching the juniors. The juniors do the clapper and the logging and stuff. The seniors will be doing the actual camerawork. There is a lot of pressure on them when we come to filming because there's so much money involved. We do have to take on kids who we know can cope with this pressure. We have to be very careful.

They come from varied backgrounds. We're a charity, we don't charge them very much because we don't want it to be elitist. You may ask how they all get on, coming from such different backgrounds. I think that the fact they are working towards one goal helps, plus they are just so committed. We have had times when the chemistry hasn't worked, but usually they get on really well. It's a good atmosphere and they don't mind being told if they're doing something wrong. There have been some major mistakes, but that's what we have to expect.

The Children's Film Unit isn't just about making the films, it's about self-awareness too, teaching kids how to work in a group, with kids they don't know from different ages, different backgrounds. It equips them with life skills which they will take away. It's something they will have for the rest of their lives. It's not marked, it's not graded, it's not an exam.

Do most of the children go on to make more films?

A lot of them want to go to film school, such as the National Film and Television School, where for every one place five hundred or so people apply. Our kids will get that place because they have worked on three or four films already. It's the first step that we give them. They find it easy to get into a film school or a college. After that they're on their own. What we do is give them a chance so they can know if it's something they want to take further. So many kids have a romantic notion of film-making and get a chance, say, when they are twenty-two. Five years later they realise that they don't really like what they are doing. At the age of eighteen our kids know whether they want to do more or not. The ones who do are just incredible. They will be the future directors and producers of the British film industry.

Colin Finbow, the director who founded the Children's Film Unit, is also the tutor and has committed his whole life to doing this. We don't get paid very much, we're not in it for the money. It is quite hard, but we have a history now. They can look back at our films and see that we know what we are doing and that the films are going to be good. If a new group goes along to a television company and asks for £100,000 to make a film I don't think they'd get it. We are in a strong position.

Channel Four have actually reduced our budget because they think we should look for co-production finance in Europe. It's ridiculous that I should have to do that. In 1992 we almost had to close down. We'd been going for ten years and suddenly our funds dried up. We had three months to raise £25,000. The *Evening Standard* stepped in, fortunately. It's crazy, after ten years. It's a unique British institution and it was going to collapse for lack of funds. However, it is thanks to Channel Four's support that we have been going for so long – I just hope it stays that way.

How do you select the children?

We can take eighty. Sometimes we have a waiting list of three hundred kids, sometimes we don't have a waiting list at all, depending if we've had recent publicity. I write to them and they have to return an application form. That puts a lot off because we ask for commitment every Saturday including school holidays. What we are doing at the moment is applying to the Arts Council for Lottery money so we can re-equip. Then we can be open on a Saturday and Sunday so we can take more kids and maybe even do some evenings. Again we need money to do that because then we would need more tutors.

That's how I'd like to expand. Then if we have two groups we could start thinking about making two films during the summer holidays at the same time. It would give more kids the opportunity because there are so many out there who want to do it and are so capable of doing it. When you first look at a film camera it can be threatening. But the kids pick it up easily like they pick up computers. You get their vision, the naiveté and the freshness that they bring to the film.

How many children's film festivals are there?

Our films go to about ten festivals, to Chicago, to Canada, Germany, Berlin. All the major children's film festivals. The films often win prizes.

That's impressive considering that at the festivals all the other films aren't made by children.

Ours are the only ones made by children. Quite often the juries don't even know that the film is made by children. We don't put it in the publicity, it's not actually stated, 'This is a film made by children.' We're in direct competition with films that are made by adults. It has to do with content, our films obviously come from kids. We're going to do a big press release on the prize we've just won. We just keep on pushing. I work here all week, Colin comes on Saturday and works from home during the week. There's an awful lot of work to do, but it's worth it.

How big are the budgets?

Willie's War was made for £108,000. It's set in 1945. All the sets were given to us. All the props we got for nothing. If it had been done for the BBC or by another company it would have cost in the region of £400,000. Most of our budgets are in that range, although I have been as low as £33,000. We couldn't do it if we weren't given the film stock for nothing, and big discounts on processing. We get a lot of support from the industry. We take a group of kids away for three weeks, they stay in dormitories and all the catering is supplied. That's how we make our film in three weeks. The schedule is very, very tight, which adds to the pressure. And every time I do it I say 'never again'.

Debbie Shuter and Adam Tysoe

'Films are sold on a thirty-second to a minute, maybe two-minute, clip. . . .'

Debbie Shuter produced *Safe Haven*, a psychological thriller set on a remote Scottish island; Adam Tysoe directed it. Both are graduates of (different) film schools and had previously worked together on documentaries. They have some interesting things to say on the nature of independent film-making, particularly on selecting the market (video, television or theatrical) at which to aim a film, and the sort of hook lines that create publicity and sales.

Adam Tysoe: Let's define 'independent'. There's independent of Hollywood. There's independent of the major studios and the major distributors. That's what a film like *Shallow Grave* is. To be truly independent is to make a film off your own back. One not financed by television or British Screen or whoever are giving out millions at the moment. *Shopping*, an 'independent film', cost a couple of million. *Shallow Grave* cost about one and a half million, not to mention the money spent on publicity.

With true independent film-making you are on your own. You don't have backing, not only in the financial sense. You develop the script on your own. There is no safety net. Only after making *Safe Haven* do I realise how vulnerable we were without that. An independent film-maker who's just starting off does not have the same experience in developing scripts as a script editor at Channel Four does. They don't have the resource of a team of intellectual minds working on the script to make it better and better and better.

It's very easy to become over-protective of your script. If you have backing, then people are giving you money. So they might be telling you what to do because of that. If you haven't got backing you've got all the freedom. Then there's a real danger that you'll end up disappearing up your own arse, which is what a lot of people do. You need people who have experience in scriptwriting and reading to look at your work. If a film is badly shot you can forgive it. But if you have script problems then the game is up really.

The danger in independent film-making is that there's no point making films if they aren't any good. Does anyone want to watch it, will anyone be engrossed in the story? As for getting a cinema release, you can't expect someone to pay (Barry Norman said this) eight quid for a ticket to go and see a film that looks like it was made for very little money and with very little expertise. It's unfair on audiences and it's not going to help the independent film world. People will say, 'I'm not going to go and see independents because they're all shite and I've wasted my Friday night and my eight quid.' Seven or eight quid is a lot of money for people to spend and they expect to be well entertained for it.

People should really think about where they're selling their film. We decided to focus on either the video market or the television market. It's being realistic about what your film can and can't achieve. I think that's the biggest problem of all. It's a hard world out there. When you've made your film, no one will take into account what you went through to make it. People will look at the film and see it for what it is. A story on a screen in front of them. Something which is very difficult to pull off. Anyone can be a film-maker, anyone can put together a film that doesn't really work, that doesn't really have a story, that doesn't really have good performances. There are so many elements you have to make work.

We shot *Safe Haven* in three and a half weeks, with one day for pick-ups and a two-day shoot in London. We had a 6:1 ratio, all unknown actors and an untested crew. Debbie was a first-time drama producer on a full-length feature and I was a first-time director. If you put yourself in that scenario, what you're effectively doing is jumping off the top of a cliff and hoping ...

Debbie Shuter: Without a parachute ...

Tysoe: ... that you're not going to hit the rocks at the bottom. There's a very small puddle of water and if you make it into that little puddle of water, you might just survive. That's what we did. I think anyone who has not directed drama and is going into it fresh is doing the same thing and shouldn't be under any illusions. It's a suicidal thing to do.

Shuter: The only reason that we did it that way is because there is no backing in this country for anyone to make films. The only way that you can get out there and make a film is just to take it all on your own back.

Let's talk about Safe Haven, *right from the beginning.*

Shuter: Last New Year we made a resolution that we were going to make our first feature. That was the end of 1993. We were developing a script, we'd written the story, written the characters. We'd commissioned a writer to write it, paid him and decided that was the film that we were going to make. Then the script came back and it was just not right; we realised it was going to be far too expensive. We went on the Dov Simens course [the twice-yearly 'Two-day Film School' held in London]. He planted in our head the idea that, if you're going to make a film, what

105

you've got to do is make a cheap film, based in one location with a few characters. We thought, 'That's a very good point there, Dov.'

The dad of this friend of ours had just bought a little Scottish island, which was perfect for the story. Four characters, one location, ideal. We wrote the treatment, wrote the character breakdown. We decided that we just didn't have the time to write the script, we aren't really writers. Our lawyer said that he had a friend who had written a lot of scripts and showed us some of the friend's work. We brought the script home, read it and thought, 'He'll do'. He lived in America, so we sent all the stuff over to him. This was at the end of January. We had a weather window to shoot in Scotland, so the shoot definitely had to be in May or June.

Have you got a sales agent?

Tysoe: We're looking, we're organising screenings. We're going to build up sales gradually, get the film to the right places, get it finished in the right way and get all the money back on the film. Our optimum aim is to sell the film and to get it seen by people. The biggest priority of all is to make sure that all our debts are paid, our investors are paid, our suppliers are paid. Hopefully, our deferrals will also get paid. If we do a big theatrical release the money, all the money, even if it does do well, is going to be soaked up. A third of it will be taken by the cinema, another third of it, minimum, will be taken by the distribution company. Twenty-five per cent of the remaining third will go to the sales agent.

Shuter: When we started *Safe Haven* we wanted it to go out theatrically. As we got further down the line we realised that there would be no point in putting it out theatrically. For one thing it would cost us a fortune. If you haven't got enough money to spend on prints and advertising, there's no point putting a film out, because no one will see it anyway.

Tysoe: There is a theory that, if you do a limited theatrical release, it gives you a vanity window, a lot of advertising, because you will get write-ups in *Time Out* and all the papers.

Shuter: As long as they're good ones, of course.

Tysoe: Even if they're not good the idea is that it creates an awareness, so that when people go down to their video store or look through the *Radio Times* they will say, 'Oh, that's a theatrical film, I'd better have a look at that.'

Shuter: It boosts television sales. That's the bottom line of what it does.

Tysoe: You have to offset that expenditure against the money you'll get from a television sale. To be quite honest you're not, unless you have a complete hit on video, going to make that money back. We're all aiming for the top, we're all aiming for the theatrical release that gets a good audience, that makes its money back, that gets really good reviews. But you have to be, when you're working in low-budget, very aware of the market-place in which you're selling your product. You have to be aware of exactly what your product is suited to. It's not even a question of good or bad. It's a question of what the film is suited to. If you're making a low-budget film, the chances are that you're a first-time film-maker, which means . . .

Shuter: . . . there are no stars in your film. All these things that we are told – sex and violence and stars sell a film – are true. For Mr Joe Bloggs reading the *Sun*, that's the kind of film he's going to go and see.

Anyway, we took the finished film to Channel Four, we showed it to their sales department. They said, 'We like it, we want to buy it, let's start talking.' Then Donald Pleasance dies. All of a sudden sales agents who have previously expressed no interest whatsoever in the film are on the phone saying, 'Let's do a deal'! They can sell it now because it's Donald Pleasance's last feature film and Miranda Pleasance's first feature film. There's a nice little hook line in there now for them. Just because we got Donald Pleasance to do a little cameo role, basically because we had cast his daughter as one of the leads. Films are not sold on how good or bad they are. Films are sold on a thirty-second to a minute, maybe two-minute, clip and a sales agent being able to say, 'Donald's last film, it's a great film, buy it!' Plus you have to make a good story, you have to make a film that looks good, you have to make a film that works.

Tysoe: The lesson is: if you're making an independent film, you're not going to sell it just like that. The chances are it's not going to work. The chances are it's all going to go wrong. You have to be aware of that, you really have to be so strongly aware of that. Because you have to have in mind that this could all go horribly wrong. There was not one moment, virtually, when I wasn't thinking, 'Jesus, we are on a knife edge here.' Right now it seems that we've got to the end of that. Things are moving upwards, but it's touch and go.

Shuter: . . . because the British fear success and people who want to be successful. They don't like people who go it alone outside the system. The Americans love it. They love people who want to go out there and do it against all odds. They love that, the British hate it. The British want you to go through the hoops. They want you to go through the ranks.

Last year, we did nothing else but *Safe Haven*. We didn't go on a holiday, we didn't go anywhere. We lived and worked out of a little council flat off the Elephant and Castle, with the film stacked up everywhere. Everywhere you looked was the film. The art department was in the bedroom. The production office was in the living room. The bathroom had props in it.

Tysoe: So you had better make sure the film you make is good. If it's not, you're going to feel suicidal at the end of it. It has to be the film that you really want to make. Otherwise you're just wasting your time. You really are, because you're not going to get any other benefits from it. I have problems with our project, it's not everything that we wanted it to be. It is what I would class as a near miss. Which is why we've been able to sell it, and why I'm sure we'll sell it again.

Shuter: It's also why we're so frustrated . . .

Tysoe: It's why it's so frustrating . . .

Shuter: Because we were that close to getting it spot on.

Tysoe: It could have been everything that we wanted it to be. Looking at the final print, you see your film up on the screen and the cuts are working, the art direction is working, the performances are working, the story is being told, people who are watching it are becoming involved. You realise when you look at it, that it looks like a film, it sounds like a film and you've done it for the amount of money that most people would spend on a few prints. Then you realise what you've achieved. It is an incredible feeling.

Charles Teton

'How can you quit from yourself?'

Charles Teton left school at sixteen to become an actor and dancer, and later an advertising photographer. He wrote, produced, directed, shot and edited *Dark Summer*, a simple urban love story set in Liverpool. The film took four years to do, spanning a year of pre-production, one location vehicle lost in the River Mersey, eighteen months filming at weekends, sixteen stitches, a dedicated Liverpool cast and crew, 300 extras and a three-year driving ban! The support of companies like Agfa-Gavaert, Rank Film Laboratories, Zonal, Sammy's, Cinequip and the North West Arts Board saw the film through six months of editing, during which the remaining rushes were used as junk spacing to economise. Despite the lack of money, Clive Chin and Augustus Pablo provided the original reggae soundtrack and the feature film has now been completed – in CinemaScope! Teton has gone on to work on *White Light*, a film based on the Four Gospels.

I started as an advertising photographer. The images I wanted to do were very anti-fashion, things that are relevant to today's society, such as men beating up their wives or girlfriends. The clothes would have nothing to do with it. The image became more of a problematic statement. Then a guy I used to work with, Roger Eaton, got a job as lighting cameraman on a really low-budget black-and-white film and asked me to help him out. I went down to the house where it was all shot. This was around the time of the great storms and it was a story based around those storms. I went down there for the shoot and left about two and a half years later because I got on so well with the director, Marcus Thompson, who was editing it himself. I was hooked by the film-making process and have been ever since.

It took us a year to edit because we ran out of money. I worked in a donkey sanctuary to raise enough money so we could eat and carry on editing. All the time I'd been pushing around the idea of *Dark Summer* in my head. I was also doing other jobs, second unit on promos and some documentaries as cameraman. I started to buy my own Arri 35mm camera, my own blimp [used to soundproof the camera], my own lights. I helped out at the Royal College of Art on four or five productions. The Arri took me a year and a half to buy because I paid for it in instalments. It was £2,500 – a lot of money. I got the lens for about a grand. My thinking was that if I got so many things I needed to make a film, I couldn't turn around and say I can't do it.

The Royal College of Art wanted to do a particular production on 35mm. They went around to all the production companies and got all their stock which was out of date. They had about 100,000 feet. In the end they chickened out and didn't use it. I took the stock and got it tested. I had the film, I had the camera, I had a rough script. I said to myself, 'I've got to do it'. I didn't look for any money from the normal sources. My reasoning was 'Who is going to give me £100,000 to make a film?' With a script that was half finished we started shooting.

Was your shoot staggered?

We did the bulk of the shoot over about ten days. I was still on the dole. I tried to get the enterprise allowance. They said, 'No way.' I was told on the quiet by one of the staff that the government had realised that they were paying writers and film-makers to make films that were slagging off the government! When I think about it now I can't really understand how we managed to do it, how we afforded to do it. Rank were brilliant to us. I went to Agfa, Rank, Sammy's, Zonal, who do sound stock, and Cinequip, the lighting company. I walked in the door and said, 'Look, I'm doing a 35mm CinemaScope film and I've got no money. Please will you help me?'

Sammy's loaned us as much gear as we wanted for eighteen months. Zonal gave us all the sound stock we needed. Cinequip loaned us lighting for practically nothing. Agfa gave us some film. *Dark Summer* was for me a way to learn really fast. I could have gone to film school, but it wouldn't have been right for me. I needed to go out there and do it, to learn by error. That's one of the best ways of learning.

How did you get people involved?

I still don't really know why people, like the suppliers, were willing to get involved. I asked them afterwards, 'Why did you help me?', and they said, 'Because we thought you were crazy!' Because I was crazy enough to do a 'scope film with no money. As for the actors and crew, I think I sparked off a dream inside them.

What kind of people were working on the set and what were they doing?

On the average shoot? I had two good lighting guys who were very dedicated. I had a sound recordist. One of the actors was also helping on the production side. The majority of the time that was it. Maybe one or two runners. The basic crew stayed, runners would come and go.

Did you ever think of quitting?

Once or twice. But how can you quit from yourself? One thing I've learnt is that before one film finishes you've got to have the rights to the book, or whatever you want to do as your next project. I've taken a year out to push this film. Okay, if I hadn't taken a year out it would have just sat on the shelf and done nothing. The first festival I went to somebody was kind enough to tell me I'd be spending a year on the festival circuit. It's another thing you learn, all part of the process of film-making. You never stop learning. You have to go out there and answer people's questions, answer the audiences' questions. They like it or they don't like it. They make you think. The next time you script a scene you think: will they understand?

To get the press coverage took me about three months. I had 400 press contacts. They got sent the blurb twice and were invited to screenings. If they didn't turn up at the screenings, then they got a video. You need to hustle them. But it shouldn't be hysterical; just calmly ring them up and check if they received the film, push a bit. I think that's why the film got so much coverage. If I'd got somebody else to do it I don't think we would have got so much coverage. I dedicated myself to making sure the press coverage was as good as it could be.

The festival circuit is a necessary evil, you need to go out there and be charming, be entertaining. I used to use the party trick of getting incredibly drunk to get over my insecurities about the film. So I got a reputation on the circuit as being a bit outrageous. The smaller festivals are better because they're very intimate, people take care of you. You go there and they pay for your drink, they pay for your food. They chaperone you, they take you to the talks they're having. It seems the smaller they are, the better they are. The bigger ones, London especially, don't take care of you; they dump you, they don't introduce you to people. We stayed away from Cannes; *Dark Summer* is too small.

The makers of Boy Meets Girl *and* The Revenge of Billy the Kid *camped outside Cannes. The makers of* Boy Meets Girl *couldn't afford to pay for a festival screening so they screened it in a restaurant.*

I didn't think it was right for our film. What I tried to do as far as the distribution and selling part of it goes was to build up a vibe about it. The press has helped that process. It's slowly building upwards instead of just being another low-budget film that has very little commercial potential. It's got an identity of its own. We've sold it in the UK: Metro Tartan have taken it on, it's had a cinema release and they're doing a video release.

111

Did you get any money for it?

I got a pittance for it but they're a good company. I was happy with the
fact that it was going with them. I think they're a respectable company.
Out of all the people you know you shouldn't trust, they're probably the
most trustworthy. Because they've got a lot to lose if they screw up,
because they're a well-respected company in the industry. I was happy
with the figure they gave me, even though it was low. I hope we'll see my
costs back. The rest of the world has yet to be sold. I haven't actively
been pushing that yet. I want them to buy the rest of the world rights
from me for cash and that's it. It may sound heartless, but I could spend
five years pushing the film around the world. I've got to go on and do the
next one.

If you have belief enough in your own work, you've got to be prepared
to sacrifice everything. That includes relationships, that includes a place
to live, that includes luxuries. That's where a lot of people stop because
they're not prepared not to live where they're living. They're not
prepared to go out and flog their CD collections because they need some
money to pay the crew on a certain day. People aren't willing to put
everything in. I think that's the difference between the people who do it
and the people who don't. I lived in absolute shit for six months. It was a
room with water dripping from the ceiling and rats outside.

Paul Hills

'The more people out there making movies, the more interest will be generated.'

Paul Hills, a member of the New Producers Alliance, was born in Tooting, south London, and was brought up in Stevenage, Hertfordshire. He wrote, produced and directed his second feature film *Boston Kickout*, a drama, with money from private investors after completing his first, *The Frontline*, which had been financed by the same people and released ... in Poland! (Paul Trijbits and Danny Cannon were executive producers on *Boston Kickout*.) He decided not to wait on TV companies and the normal avenues of finance to make the film he wanted to make.

You've only just finished shooting Boston Kickout.

Yes, last Sunday. There was a scene that we had to pick up because we weren't allowed to film it where the film was set. It was a car ramming through the window of a shop. It's a rites of passage film about four young boys growing up in an English new town in Hertfordshire, what happens to them over the course of a summer, how they go their separate ways.

How did you get the film together?

I'd done shorts. I'd produced something at the National Film and Television School, done pop promos, small documentaries and other bits and pieces. I did a full-length film on 16mm about three years ago called *The Frontline*, which was set in London and Manchester. That really helped this along, I suppose. Having said that, *The Frontline* was a commercial failure.

Did you actually get it released?

It's gone out all over Poland! It's been over Poland many times. But it's very uncommercial because it's such a bleak story. It's depressing all the way through, it's got the words 'fuck' and 'cunt' all through it, so no TV station wanted to touch it. At one point we were going to sell it to Granada. But they pulled out. So it became a calling card really.

Are you using the same producer?

Yeah. Myself! *The Frontline* was a nightmare to be honest. It was three years of constant aggro because I wrote, produced, directed, edited and designed it and it went on for ever. I'm still paying off the bills now.

How much money did you manage to raise for it?

Twelve grand. That was enough. Eighty-six minutes on 16mm.

How many people were working on Boston Kickout?

Before I hadn't done anything with more than twenty-five people in the crew. For this one we had fifty or something.

Were any of the investors people who'd invested in The Frontline?

There was one investor who'd invested in *The Frontline* and had lost his money. We approached him with *Boston Kickout*. He put money into it, considerably more money into it. He has faith in me, I suppose. He must have. Still, it was a long trek getting the crew together, getting the cast together, all that kind of thing. Obviously with a low-budget movie, getting the best people is always a problem. Having Paul Trijbits and Danny Cannon executive producing it helped.

Do you feel you're part of a revival in independent film-making in this country?

A lot of things are happening in and around the New Producers Alliance. It's really a great feeling. People are going out there and making movies. They're not waiting on TV companies and the normal avenues of finance to come through or sitting around waiting for the telephone to ring. Low-budget deferred-payment films have been going on in the States for years. Anything to get people out there making movies is good. The more people out there making movies, the more interest will be generated. More people going to see movies will generate more movies being made. It may be new in this country but in America they've been making independent films since the year dot.

How did you feel coming up to the first shoot?

I felt more stressed on the night before the first day of shooting than I'd ever felt in my life. I couldn't concentrate on anything apart from the set-ups, the shots, the lenses.

How did you approach shooting on the first day?

I tried to shoot it as chronologically as possible. It was a long day, eighteen hours, twenty-seven set-ups; trying to make it look sunny when it was raining.

Would you describe the role of line producer?

Well a line producer makes sure things are kept on budget and on schedule, things like that. I had worked with the line producer before, as a focus-puller. I was in Manchester, looking for a focus-puller. I saw him and he had a couple of references and I phoned up the references and they said he was brilliant, but it was all bullshit. At the end of the movie he told me that he'd never pulled focus before and I thought 'this guy has balls'. We've been friends since then. He told me that he was so scared on the first day that he'd be found out. It just proves you can do anything if you put your mind to it.

So where did you get your money?

It's from private investors and companies who have a large portfolio of cash and who want to diversify their interests. Filming is high risk. All the money is from outside the UK. There's no English money in the film at all.

Michael Hakata

'Our budget is the kind that most films would have as their catering budget!'

Michael Hakata was born in Zimbabwe and moved to Britain in 1974. He discovered film when he saw *Star Wars* and discovered the art of film when he saw *Un chien andalou*. When he talked to Graham Jones he was just about to shoot *Two Bad Mice*, his first feature. Since shooting the film he has backed away from the deal with the distribution company Screen Edge mentioned in the interview, but has had considerable interest from other distributors. In a letter to the editors of this book, he writes that if there's one thing everyone wants to do in the UK, it's to make more films. He had tremendous support from the British film industry – the labs, camera companies and studios, as well as complete dedication and enthusiasm from his cast and crew. In the end the film was shot for £15,000 in fifteen days! He is now writing more scripts and developing other projects.

We started with just an idea for a film. Then we wrote the script. I wrote the first draft, talked about it with Joel Martin, my collaborator, then we went into more detail together, starting with the story structure, and wrote the story. The characters came with it. We took the script to sales agents, to distributors, to production companies and to actors. Almost instantly we started to get comeback from crew experts saying, 'This is a good project, we want to get involved.' This is the way it happens. Without that collaborative thing you're lost. We're learning the ropes as we go along. The more people get involved, the more they bring their expertise and show us where we're going wrong and move us in new directions.

When we were auditioning cast we found loads of actors. Either they've been out of work for years and are brilliant, and you can't understand why they're not working. Or they were new actors, who just blew us away. The auditions were pretty positive. That was about the end of December 1994. I have put in a lot of rehearsal time, rather than deciding just to turn up on set and shoot to get into the characters. One thing you find with a lot of film-making at the moment, particularly in a lot of independent films from this country, is that they're losing character, losing a sense of character motivation. Films lack rounded characters. So what you end up having is a shallow film where you don't really care about the characters.

What format are you shooting on?

We're shooting on Super 16 which we're then going to blow up to 35mm, when we get the money. Today we got a distribution deal with a company who've been distributing music videos and things for a long time and who are now moving into feature films by setting up a video label. They read the script and said they loved it. Our film *Two Bad Mice* should be one of the first films they'll have on the shelves, which is quite a plus. They just do video. But today we also got a letter from a big cinematic distributor, who said that they want to distribute when we have a completed product. They're saying that they love the script but they won't say anything more than that until it's actually finished. They're certainly taking it into a whole new realm that we weren't even thinking about.

When we started, we already had cast and crew on board but no money. It was so nerve-wracking that over Christmas I actually thought I was going to get an ulcer. I couldn't sleep, I couldn't eat. I had a shitty Christmas; the turkey was going cold in front of me. I was just cacking myself. Because by now, we'd gone too far, there were too many people. If we had let them down at that point, then we would have had no career in any part of the industry. But we're still pinching ourselves, we can't believe it. There is still a lot of stuff we haven't got yet, like camera equipment. We've got a very tight budget and we're trying to be creative and business-minded at the same time, which we don't really want to be. I'm working at the moment where I don't want to be, for a facilities house, just to get money. Every night when I finish work I'm over to the office and I start living the alter-ego life of a film-maker.

Our budget is the kind that most films would have as their catering budget! Half the stuff has been donated, or given at seriously cheap prices, which involves loads of negotiating with people. What we have will barely get us through. I won't tell you the exact amount; it's thousands, but not a lot of them. That's problematic.

What do you have to get done before the first day of shooting?

Pulling everyone together. We're going to have our first full crew meeting on Monday evening. Everyone – make-up, set design, runners, gaffers, lighting, camera – is going to get together and talk about how we're going to pull off a twelve-day shoot. A twelve-day shoot like this will probably make the *Guinness Book of Records*. In the next two and a bit weeks, we will have more rehearsals with actors. We don't want people to turn up on set and say, 'Can I try this approach?' and 'Sorry, I fucked that up', because we haven't got the stock. We're shooting on a ratio of 3:1, which is tiny. We're not a big production. People will turn up on set, they'll be walking around in the character's shoes. They'll know their role so well, it'll be blocked so well and choreographed so well they'll just step into the shoes. It'll be one-take wonders all the way. Long takes too, because we can't do loads of set-ups either.

We're spending this Sunday looking at a load of movies for cutting style. Once you get in the cutting room it can change the whole thing. A lot of things can't be done until something else has been done. For example, the set designer has got to get her list of props and say how she's going to dress the set, otherwise the director of photography won't know how to light it. The main thing is the shooting schedule, so we know what we're doing every day. We're not going to ad-lib, which is why good pre-production is everything on a film. Whatever happens, nothing can stop it. With that attitude, we'll get it made. Even though the distributors have only seen the script and we haven't signed any contracts, they've said that we have got a deal.

How much does that count for?

They've given us a few things as acts of good faith. There's one scene where there's a montage of various film clips. They have a back catalogue of videos, and they gave us a whole wad that we're editing together for one of the scenes. A hundred pounds' worth of videos. I doubt they would have given that to us if they weren't interested. But they've no financial proof that we've got a budget or that we're not going to run off with the money. So it's all trust and being on the same level. Visionary, or their video label, Screen Edge, are going on about having a punk ethic, renegade, making up rules as you go along. Which is exactly what we're doing.

Their idea about the punk ethic is that the film industry is not at present similar to the independent record industry, where little companies are creating music. But it should be, it's the same thing, but music with light. Instead of big companies saying what you have to do, and that you have to follow them otherwise you're not going to get the cash and you're not going to get the distribution, which is most important. They're willing to take risks, as long as the films have that punk ethic, as long as there's an edge to them. Which is why they're called Screen Edge.

So what had you done before?

I've been working crappy jobs in the film industry for a few years and getting nowhere. Working up those ladders is not my thing. I've been writing for those years as well. I've written around ten scripts. I'm not a very good salesperson. So instead of trying to sell these scripts, which are quite oddball anyway, we've decided to make the thing. Then people will trust it and understand it. With me the script is a process. It carries on being written, it's going to be written right up to the shoot. Everyone who has read it has loved it. It's probably the best script I've written, although I wrote two scripts back to back. The one I wrote before this I'm hoping to make straight after this.

Eric Fellner

'I'm not just going to make one film and hope it's a masterpiece....'

Eric Fellner produced *Sid and Nancy* in 1985 and then went on to produce films such as *Pascali's Island, Liebestraum* and *Hidden Agenda.* In 1993 he executive produced *Four Weddings and a Funeral.* Since then Working Title have released *French Kiss, Panther, Moonlight and Valentino* and, more recently, *Dead Man Walking, Fargo* and *Loch Ness,* on all of which he was executive producer.

My journey began when I was eighteen and only interested in movies and music, so I fought to get a job as a runner on music videos. In 1980 it was a very new business. There were two or three directors in the world making music videos. I was lucky enough to get a job with a guy who ran his own company. He had his own cameras, his own sound equipment, his own cutting rooms, his wife was the cameraman and producer and they produced everything from home. If he got a call on a Friday night about a shoot he didn't have to call anyone. It was a fantastic way to learn, to be given a camera and told to go out and shoot, to be given footage and told to sync it up and edit it.

I had a year of learning a little bit about every aspect of film-making, editing, camera and sound. I hadn't gone to university or film school, I just had a layman's desire to do it. After this there was nothing more for me to learn without starting to specialise.

I decided that the aspect of film-making which most interested me and I could achieve quickly was to be a producer. So I offered to work for another music video producer for two months for free. At the time they were producing videos for Ultravox, Spandau Ballet, David Bowie, etc. After two months with this company I knew so much about what was going on on a day-to-day basis that they couldn't fire me.

Then one of the producers left the company and suddenly I found myself, eighteen months into the film business, being asked by the top two music video directors in the country to produce their music videos. It went very well. During the next four years I produced over a hundred videos and at the end I felt I'd learnt as much as I could. I wanted to move on to become a 'real' producer.

So I sold my company and figured I had enough money to live on for nine months. I sat down at home with my telephone, bought a copy of *Spotlight* and called all the theatrical and writer's agents. I'd never met a writer or an actor before, but I had now decided I was a film producer and that I wanted to meet as many of them as possible. Through an agent friend of mine, Nicky Hart, I met Alex Cox. I was now three months into my nine months of money. He had the script for *Sid and Nancy*, which at that time was called *Love Kills*. He was a maverick, he didn't want to work with someone who knew what they were doing and he liked the fact that I had loads of energy. I budgeted it, and I told him we needed £2.5 million. He said that was fine; I should go ahead and raise the money. He said he wouldn't give me an 'option', which didn't bother me as I didn't know what an 'option' was.

I thought that someone would give me a cheque for £2.5 million and we'd go and make the film, but I soon learnt that it doesn't work like that. There were endless negotiations and contracts and God knows what. With constant support from Margaret Matheson and Scott Meek at Zenith, we got the money and suddenly I was a film producer. The first day I walked on to the set of *Sid and Nancy* was the first day I'd ever been on a real film set with actors and live sound. It brought home to me that if you want to do it, you just do it. You just have to be relatively smart and dedicated and have an interest in what it is you're trying to do. If you are prepared to put the time and effort in you can be a film producer. It's not rocket science, but it *is* demanding.

The problem of being an independent producer and having no back-up is that you have to have blinkers on to get the film made. You spend so much time trying to get it financed, trying to get distribution, trying to get your actors, that you actually don't have the time that you really would like to have to put into working with the director, working with the screenplay, developing it to the right stage. You can't actually enjoy the process of making the film. You're constantly worried that you're going to go over budget, that the bond company is going to take over, or whether the financiers and the distributors are going to be happy with the film at the end of the day.

It's a very, very tough thing to be. At the same time, if there's ever a problem you're the first one they ask to defer your fee. What the independent producers mustn't forget is that it's not called the film world, or the film culture, or the film art, it's the film business. To think that we're any different to any other business is to go in with the wrong attitude. If you want to go in on a cultural level, then work with low budgets. There's nothing wrong with that. But don't start trying to raise £10 million for your cultural foray.

A lot of the time producers don't understand distribution, they don't understand marketing, they don't understand the market-place. I'm only getting to grips with it now because I have the same distributors,

PolyGram, who distribute all our movies. The same marketing people market them and the same financiers finance them. I don't have to spend so much time trying to lock down this, that and the other for each film.

When I was on my own making films as an independent producer and saw them on to third-party distributors, everything that happened from the minute we finished the film had nothing to do with me or the director. They made all the decisions; they decided what the poster was going to look like; they decided who it was going to go out to; they decided how much money was going to be spent on it; they decided what the marketing campaign was; they decided if it would get released at all; when, how and where it would get released.

But once you have some control you can then dictate how your film is released and how it's going to work. It's just a learning process, you've got to look at it as a career. I'm in the film business, I'm a producer and that's my career and I'm going to do it for twenty years or whatever. I'm not just going to make one film and hope it's a masterpiece, I'm going to learn on every picture. For ever and ever I'm going to be learning. On a creative level, on a distribution level, on a financial level.

From *Sid and Nancy* I went on to produce nine other films, some great, some not so great, but all of which gave me enormous satisfaction. I was lucky enough to work with some very talented people who through their films gave me some fantastic experiences. Three years ago I formalised an agreement with Tim Bevan and Working Title. PolyGram bought the company, which is when I went from being a true indie producer to being more of a corporate 'animal', producing and supplying films for one distributor. Since then we've made twelve films including *Four Weddings and a Funeral*. It's amazing that a $4 million film can generate $250 million at the box-office. But that's the beauty of this business – you just never know ...

Simon Sprackling and Tim James

'Because of our education system, we have this idea that out there, beyond all this, is the person who will help me.'

Simon Sprackling directed *Funny Man*. Tim James co-produced it and took the part of the Funny Man. They first worked together on *Augustine*, a National Film and Television School production. Since then they have banded together to work on *Vermin* and the sequel to *Funny Man*, *Funny Man 2: Funny Man Goes to Hollywood*. They are firm believers in doing it for yourself, realising that no one else out there can make your film happen apart from you!

Simon Sprackling: My personal journey has been one of a failed relationship with the education system. My school career was a nightmare, useless. I got slung out. I got interested in music and was in bands and so forth. I moved from Bristol and came down to London when I was about seventeen. I started squatting, mucking about and doing things that you should do when you're that age.

There was a very rich music scene in London at the end of the 70s. Pop videos started around then. In the early 80s I found that there was a unit set up to do Super 8 and 16mm film-making in the East End of London, which was where I was living at the time. It was free if you were on the dole, or a couple of quid, or something like that. I wanted to do some videos for our band. So I went along to learn. It was very good, they didn't really hassle you about anything. They just gave you the camera and told you to fuck off and enjoy yourself.

I did a lot of silly things, and then it spilled over and I wasn't doing things just to do with the band. I started going off to amateur boxing nights and stuff like that in the East End. Filming seven-year-old kids beating the shit out of each other, encouraged by their parents, which I thought was really funny. So I got into using the camera. Then I realised I was more interested in that than the music. I decided that I needed another educational establishment to learn more. I couldn't get into film school, because they weren't really interested in seeing my Super 8 films or anything like that. I decided a communications course might be similar. You know, they have TV rooms and equipment.

I managed to find some appalling small college in Edinburgh which would take me. It appealed because of the strong arts base that they had up there, the festival and stuff. I knew the licensing laws were very lenient there as well, so I thought, 'That'll suit me as a city to go to!' So I got there, and the usual thing happened: you turn up at the college and what they show you in the brochure is the stuff you can't use. You discover that the equipment is for the technicians, not for you. But I managed to find some very old equipment that they didn't use.

I'd got another band together while I was there and I carried on doing the videos for them. Then I got slung out of the college because I didn't do any work. I was just making little films and not doing any of the work I was supposed to be doing. Eventually I realised if I wanted to get anything done, I'd have to come back to London. So I moved back in about 1989 and met up with an old mate of mine. He was working as an outside producer for the National Film and Television School on somebody's graduation film. I agreed to production manage the film for him. What I noticed when we were doing this thing with the National Film and Television School was that there was a shortage of doers around the place. There were a lot of thinkers, but not enough bloody doers.

Tim James: There were a lot of dour people.

[To Tim James] So what had you been doing before making Funny Man?

James: Just before I'd been sailing across the Atlantic in a yacht and diving for treasure in the Caribbean. That involves some degree of doing, and very quickly. If your sail breaks and your boat tips over you've got to act pretty quickly.

What kind of performance work had you done before?

James: I trained as an actor at the Welsh College of Music and Drama for three years. After that I did the usual thing you do after leaving drama school: set up a landscaping company. Then I came to London and set up a theatre company with Simon's brother whom I'd met at drama school. I realised it was far easier to perform to kids and tour in theatres than it was to dig holes in the ground. We continued like that for a while. Then we got offered a job in the West Indies. So we went out there for a couple of years. I came back and got back involved in *Augustine*, which was being made at the National Film and Television School.

Sprackling: Making *Augustine* with people from the film school who had been trained in the appropriate way, we became conscious that they couldn't organise a piss-up in a brewery. We were fundamental to making the film happen and we weren't really getting a lot of thanks for it. We came off the back of *Augustine* with the knowledge that we had the ability between the three of us to get something on the road. We decided we were going to do something. From the point of making that decision the thing started to come together. I knew I had to go away and write something, and I gave myself a week to do it.

James: Suddenly people started falling out of the woodwork, phoning up saying, 'I've heard you're filming, can I come help?'

Sprackling: We discovered how much we enjoyed the process of making films. It was a pleasure for us; there was no real pain. Or the pain was part of the entertainment. We'd also developed a number of personal contacts with facilities houses and film processors, so they knew who we were. We were able to go to Technicolor. Because they knew us, they wanted to know what we were up to. We outlined our plan and said: 'Would you come in and back us by giving us a deal whereby we don't have to pay any money for your services for a long time?' They liked us. I think a lot of people had trust in us. We made a short version of the film, where we established the character of Funny Man. We took it to the film markets to get ourselves a sales agent.

How much money did you have for the little one?

Sprackling: For the little one we had about eight grand. We had shot a pop video for somebody who paid us five grand. So we incorporated the shooting of the pop video into making our own promo, which brought in £5,000. Then we used the £5,000 plus another £3,000 we were able to get our hands on. What was quite fundamental to getting the film made was its low British humour, which I think was appreciated by a lot of people running the facilities houses. They were willing to go with it because they liked it. Unlike the kind of people working at British Screen. I'm pretty sure we'd have got a letter back from them saying, 'This is appalling, I wouldn't dream of giving you any money for it.' But a company in the business, like Technicolor, were willing to offer us substantial credit.

James: Some of these people, especially people working for lighting companies who have come up from being electricians and sparks, are particularly difficult to deal with. Their main concern is that their boys get sorted. Some of them will not help you in the slightest because they think, 'Who are you, you stupid little fucking upstart, coming into my office, thinking you can make a film when I've been here all these years?'

One particular guy, the head of a particular lighting company, very emphatically told me that deferred films have never worked, they never fucking would work and that I was wasting my – and his – fucking time. I remember standing up, banging my fist on his desk and getting very angry, looking him straight in the face, being so close to him that I could have nutted him. Then he said that he knew I was serious and got out a bottle of wine and offered me a drink. I'd been up most of the night, it was now two o'clock in the afternoon – I was waiting for my breakfast. But when he said, 'Do you want a drink?', and I said 'Yeah', it was important because he felt he'd gone that extra mile with me. He was prepared to commit to something, because he could see my commitment. We made a deal.

Sprackling: When making a low-budget film, you've got a mixed-ability group of people. That is the fact of the matter. If you're not paying the money, you cannot have anything other than a mixed-ability group. What happens over the process of production is that you find out who's who. Over the first week you get walk-outs. You get people who go, saying, 'I can't fucking handle this', and break down. All this shit happens. You get the people who nobody likes on the shoot, who can't handle it, the people who talk the talk but can't walk the walk, who crack up, who can't handle the hours. Over the first week of shooting it sorts itself out. You find out who can do what.

James: People get repositioned.

We had one mention on some TV programme, it was the *Big E*. They showed a very good clip, which was great for us. The next day people tracked us down to the location, or phoned us up. There was even a guy from Brighton who called us up. He had his own small production company with video cameras and so on, and he offered to be a runner as well as filming some of the production. We had a slot on his late-night TV show. He was prepared to drive under his own steam, we didn't pay him anything at all.

I think there are a lot of people in the UK who want to be involved.

Sprackling: Well, certainly people start to come out of the woodwork once you're going and it's happening. There are so many people who want to be involved. We even got people just rolling up with their gear saying, 'Can you use us?' One of the things that I thought interesting was that some people had done a lot of work on adverts. They were used to working with a lot of money and lots of cups of tea. A very well-paid industry, never a money problem, never a logistical problem. They're used to walking up to the production department and saying, 'I need this, can you order it for me?' When they came to us and said that in the course of production, and we said, 'No, here's a piece of string and a piece of wood, make it', they couldn't handle it. A lot of them coming from that angle freaked out and left in tears. They just couldn't handle the idea of 'Work it out, I don't care how you do it, just get it done.'

What do you think of the New Producers Alliance and the First Film Foundation?

Sprackling: I think First Film's complete bollocks, I've got no time for that organisation. It's about groups of people who are given jobs because they're the right people, part of the soft left. I don't buy into that. What's the other one?

The New Producers Alliance.

Sprackling: I don't really understand that. I've got a nasty suspicion it might be a grumbling shop.

They've got 700 members now. It's £30 for a producer and £55 for a director to join. They set up seminars, which are pretty good. It seems to be independent producers getting together.

Sprackling: I think it's a way of saying you're a producer without making a film. You only have to pay some money and you're a producer, but you don't have to make a film. There's only one way to become a producer, a film producer as opposed to a television producer. You have to get money to make films. That's it.

It may be good because it's getting people together.

Sprackling: The good thing is you can choose if you want to join it. I don't think as a lobbying organisation it'll ever do anything. If the massed ranks can't get any change out of the government, how can the New Producers Alliance? I am a naturally cynical person.
James: You sit down with a blank bit of a paper and a pencil, or a telephone and a blank bit of paper. You get on the phone and start calling people. The only way is to talk to people. If the New Producers Alliance get you to talk to people like sales agents and distributors, then fine. Ultimately, you're just one of many people and you have to cultivate these relationships yourself.
Sprackling: You require all the positive energy you can muster. You mustn't dissipate it. I meet very young producers around the place who want to get things together with a load of us. I just say to them, 'Why are you dissipating your energy?' We aren't a group of people. I place a bet that for every person in the New Producers Alliance who says in a bar 'I'm glad those lads did *Funny Man*' there are more saying 'I'm fucking glad they failed.' This is a bitching industry. There are people I want to see fail. Don't have any illusions about that.

There is no great thing – we aren't all mates together. It isn't like that. Save your energy, concentrate in one place, get your film made. That's all that fucking matters. The rest is having a pint, that's all it is, it's just chit-chat. We're firmly of the school of 'Do it!' It is a solitary activity. From out of nowhere this thing happens. It's an event, it happens once. It's about creating those moments. Not attempting to join these individual moments together for some sort of broad story, because it doesn't exist.

You got your money from the City, family and friends. Could you break that down?

Sprackling: We got twenty grand from a guy in the City. Ten grand from the guy who did the music. The other twenty grand patched together from bits and pieces. There was another five grand from a girl we knew in the City as well.

James: The production manager put five grand in. He just got an overdraft and stuck some money in, because he thought it was a good idea.

Talking about a journey is never any substitute for putting one foot in front of the other.

Sprackling: You need experience. Although our story may have similarities to others, it won't be the same as somebody else's. It'll never be the same as that moment when you've got to make the decision. When you have a rock there and a hard place there and you've got to choose between the two. There is no substitute for that moment. That's probably why we're a little slow to support this whole move to bring people together. I'm not sure we're bringing people together for the right reasons.

Because of our education system, we have this idea that out there, beyond all this, is the person who will help me. We've just got to find them. They will see our genius and that'll be the moment. I call it 'The Sending Your Script to David Puttnam School of Film-making'. David will recognise my genius, the rest will be gravy. This person does not exist. The quicker you take that on board ... No, sorry, they do exist. That person does exist. That person is yourself. It isn't out there, it's in here. When you've grasped that, it all starts to make sense.

Index